Language Policy

Language Policy

A SLIM GUIDE

Florian Coulmas

OXFORD
UNIVERSITY PRESS

Great Clarendon Street, Oxford, OX2 6DP,
United Kingdom

Oxford University Press is a department of the University of Oxford.
It furthers the University's objective of excellence in research, scholarship,
and education by publishing worldwide. Oxford is a registered trade mark of
Oxford University Press in the UK and in certain other countries

Published in the United States of America by Oxford University Press
198 Madison Avenue, New York, NY 10016, United States of America

British Library Cataloguing in Publication Data

Data available

Library of Congress Control Number: 2024947059

ISBN 9780192874214
ISBN 9780192874269 (pbk.)

DOI: 10.1093/9780191976377.001.0001

Printed and bound by
CPI Group (UK) Ltd, Croydon, CR0 4YY

The manufacturer's authorised representative in the EU for product safety is
Oxford University Press España S.A. of El Parque Empresarial San Fernando de Henares, Avenida de Castilla, 2 – 28830 Madrid (www.oup.es/en or
product.safety@oup.com). OUP España S.A. also acts as importer into Spain
of products made by the manufacturer.

Contents

List of figures and tables

1

Why language policy?

'Long before shots were fired, a linguistic power struggle was playing out in Ukraine.'[1]

"'A generational shift': war prompts Ukrainians to embrace their language.

Until last year Kyiv was largely a Russian-speaking city. A survey in January revealed that since Putin's invasion a year ago, 33 per cent of Kyivans have adopted the Ukrainian language. About 46 per cent said they had been speaking Ukrainian for a long time. Another 13 per cent remain Russian speakers."[2]

"When Ukrainian defence forces encounter a suspected Russian saboteur passing himself off as a Ukrainian, they usually ask him to say the Ukrainian word for a type of local bread: *palyanitsya*. Almost invariably the suspect betrays his nationality and politics by pronouncing it with a different ending: *palyanitsa*."[3]

Nothing testifies to humanity's (partial) liberation from the law of the jungle more clearly than the ability to resolve hostilities peacefully. Language is the tool of doing this. Can we even imagine how non-violent conflict resolution could be accomplished without language; how causes of tensions can be identified; alternative perspectives compared; solutions considered, modified, proposed, and compromises reached? The art of conversation is not only an evolutionary advantage that sets us apart from other animals; it also fuelled the evolution of our species more than any other capacity. Arguments and counterarguments, symbolic representation, understanding and

Language Policy. Florian Coulmas, Oxford University Press. © Florian Coulmas (2025).
DOI: 10.1093/9780191976377.003.0001

accommodating another point of view instead of the survival of the fittest. Language: the instrument of concord.

This is what language in the abstract sense enables us to do. But *our* language is a concrete system, and the best one of all the many that exist. Since written records do not reach back very far, it is impossible to say when humans started using language to put others down. However, that people cherish their language and consider it superior to the uncouth tongues of others is certainly an old story. Slight differences in pronunciation were used from earliest times to distinguish, discriminate, and bully outsiders, and could even be regarded as a legitimate reason to put them to death, as recounted, for instance, in the Old Testament story of *shibboleth* (Judges 12: 2–6). Or take the Greek word *logos*—from which 'logic'—which in ancient times meant 'language' and 'reason', inviting the conclusion that those whose proficiency in Greek was imperfect or non-existent were stupid barbarians deserving to be excluded. Language: the banner of discord.

Language is both our unrivalled means of creating understanding and harmony, and a source of discrimination and hostility. This inherent functional contradiction between the cognitive and the emotional, between language as principal means of conflict settling and a prominent reason of conflict emergence, is at the heart of language policy. Universal medium for the expression of reason, on one hand, and object of sentimental attachment, on the other, language lends itself to both inclusion and exclusion. The lines that can be drawn on the basis of languages are not fixed and the two functions or dimensions—what is said and how it is said—are not always held apart, which increases the complexity of language as a subject of politics, and that of language policy (LP) as a subject of research.

Language policy is nothing new. Consider what two and a half thousand years ago Confucius (551–479 BCE) thought about language and government. When asked what he would do if he had to govern the country, as reported in the *Analects*, he famously replied: 'If something has to be put first, it is, perhaps, the rectification of names' (Confucius 1992: 223). He was deeply convinced that without language being properly regulated, state and society would sink into chaos. For

> when names are not correct, what is said will not sound reasonable; when what is said does not sound reasonable, affairs will not culminate in success; when affairs do not culminate in success, rites and music will not flourish; when rites and music do not flourish, punishments will not be exactly right; when punishments are not exactly right, the common people will not know where to put hand and foot (Confucius 1992: 121).

In a similar vein, Plato (420s–347 BCE) emphasized the importance of language to politics. In the dialogue *Phaedrus*, he has Socrates explain that

> The first rule of good speaking is to know and speak the truth; as a Spartan proverb says, 'true art is truth'; whereas rhetoric is an art of enchantment, which makes things appear good and evil, like and unlike, as the speaker pleases. Its use is not confined, as people commonly suppose, to arguments in the law courts and speeches in the assembly; it is rather a part of the art of disputation. [. . .] If we do not know the truth, we can neither make the gradual departures from truth by which men are most easily deceived, nor guard ourselves against deception (Plato 2005: 9).

Aristotle (384–322 BCE) described humans as political animals endowed with

> the power of speech [which] is intended to set forth the expedient and inexpedient, and therefore likewise the just and the unjust. And it is a characteristic of man that he alone has any sense of good and evil, of just and unjust, and the like, and the association of living beings who have this sense makes a family and a state (Aristotle 1964: 8).

The echo of these early pronouncements about the political significance of language resounds through the ages, as, to give just one more example, in Cardinal Richelieu's (1585–1642 CE) remark, 'if the language is corrupted, the political system is corrupt' (Robitaille 2002: 49).

In the age of alternative facts and fake news, this sounds hardly out of date. Because of the universal nature of language there is continuity; however, because of the parochial nature of politics the concerns of language policy change in tune with social, economic, and international developments. This *Slim Guide* is designed to give an overview of contemporary language policy issues with some historical background wherever that is helpful for understanding.

Based on a set of values and ideas, language policy concerns the multitude of human languages and the actual language practices of the members of a relevant community. Such a community can be large or small. At the high end, all-encompassing organizations such as the United Nations and its affiliates, which represent all of humanity, have language policies and, at the lower end, the family is a social unit that can decide on a language policy. Between these two there are various polities, levels of administration, institutions, and agencies that have language norms explicitly or implicitly grounded in language policies. For some time, only the nation state was thought to be responsible for language policy, but as this field of study progressed it became clear there are other agents that are subordinate to it or independent of it. This is because language norms are a crucial aspect of institutional norms. While the historical references above suggest that this has been so throughout history, in modern times, especially in train with decolonization when the present world order took shape, language norms have become an object of intense interest in politics and therefore in science. Language norms are part of the power structure of nation states, federal states, municipalities, companies, as well as institutions such as parliaments, ministries, city governments, schools, courts of law, healthcare offices, and government bodies relating to borders, immigration, and customs, among others. They regulate, for example, which languages may be used for teaching, legal procedures, application letters, election posters, and ballot papers, etc., the value accorded to a language as a tool of governance, and the language(s) that are compatible with or best suited for the institutional goals. And some of them are tasked with aspects of language policy that are sometimes called 'language planning' or 'language management', that is, with the setting of standards and efforts to make some or all members of a speech community change their ways of speaking and move in the normatively prescribed direction.

Language norms may be adhered to unquestioningly or challenged. Consider cities where recent demographic developments have created ethnolinguistic enclaves. Consider schools in which a growing proportion of pupils do not speak the dominant language or do not speak it adequately. In such situations, norm defenders and reformers may face each other turning the extant language regime and proposed amendments into political issues. What these examples imply is that immigration—as we know, a defining feature of the twenty-first century—is one of the dynamics that has put language on the agenda of many institutions in many places, as well as for many families. As migrants themselves or having a migration background they may choose various strategies for acquiring the dominant language or maintaining their heritage language(s). Compulsory education and the increased importance of access to information for everyday life have transformed language use from a default condition into a matter of domain-specific choice. For both families and institutions language choice is subject to values, ideologies, and goals.

For families, language choice is about balancing integration, tradition, and, often enough, career prospects. For institutions it is about effective governance, providing quality services, and, in some cases, exercising symbolic domination. In any case, linguistic heterogeneity is the frame condition which in modern societies has much to do with participation in social, political, and economic life; and it is the interweaving of social, political, and economic properties of languages that make language policy an important and sometimes explosive issue in contemporary society.

Family language policy is limited to language practices in a sphere with which those concerned are familiar. For language policies on a broader scale this is not necessarily the case. Do you/those in charge of education and municipal administration know how many languages are spoken in Sidney, Buenos Aires, New Delhi? A well-informed language policy therefore starts out from an ethnographic or sociolinguistic description of the actual situation that comprises languages, varieties, demographics, social hierarchies, and institutions that are deliberately charged with setting language norms, or norms for communication in general, or have evolved to do so spontaneously in the course of socio-political development. What are the roles of the various languages and varieties in the community? When is the dominant/official/national language used, in speech and writing? In which language(s) is school education available? What are the preferences for the language of instruction in schools? How useful is a language in the labour market? Is there a generally accepted lingua franca? Is bilingualism widespread? What is the literacy rate? Are there recognizable social patterns of it? Are there any frictions between language groups? Seeking answers to these and similar questions is indispensable for realistic language policy making on national and local levels. This seems obvious enough, but for ideological and other reasons that will be discussed throughout this book, it is not easy to achieve always and everywhere, which is yet another challenge language policy poses for those executing and studying it. Generally speaking, language policies comprise prescriptions, proscriptions, and permissions, such as, for example:

> Constitutional texts are established in French, in Dutch, and in German.
>
> In 1967, the use of Chinese in schools and public activities was banned in Indonesia by presidential order.
>
> The rules of procedure provide that in court, if a witness does not have a sufficient command of the official language, his or her testimony may be given in the courtroom in his or her own language and a translation be provided.

The many existing institutions and organizations currently entrusted with developing, implementing, and monitoring such regulations indicate that language policy is more important than ever today. This is reflected in the fact that language policy has become an academic discipline with its own literature of journals and handbooks (cf., e.g., Spolsky 2012; Tollefson and Pérez-Milans 2018). Subsequent chapters cover the major subfields of it beginning with a brief description of important concepts and theoretical approaches. The discussion then proceeds to language conflicts that have accompanied modernization and still frame language policy issues around the world, as illustrated at the outset of this chapter. How languages are made objects of political regimentation and who the agents of such processes are is discussed, as well as the underlying ideologies which also and especially affect school education (language-in-education policy). Policy matters that have attracted much attention in recent decades are dealt with in three chapters about international language regimes, the economy of language, and language policy implications of migration. The final two chapters are about two other topics that have come to the fore in recent decades, the endangerment of numerically minor languages and language regulation in the context of and motivated by anti-discrimination policies relating to race, national origin, sex, gender, language, religion, or any other status.

Politics and political decision making have been an integral part of social life since antiquity, and language has been part of it. But political science is a relatively young discipline that arose in modern times in the late nineteenth century. As a field of scientific research, language policy is even younger, having begun to take shape in the 1960s (Ricento 2000). One way of scientifically examining the complexity of policy making is to break it down into stages. A scheme for this, introduced by Harold Lasswell (1956) and widely used in political science, is known as the 'policy cycle model'. An idealized heuristic model it is designed to explain how policy decisions are made, what stages the process usually goes through, what the available policy tools are and who the interested participants are. It identifies the objectives of the policymaker, the policies to achieve these objectives, the concrete actions to be employed, and the resources to implement and evaluate/adjust the policy. Of the fields to which the policy cycle model can be applied, language policy is one. The model depicted in Figure 1 is adapted from Climent-Ferrando (2023). Other varieties identify six rather than four stages: agenda setting, formulation adoption, implementation, evaluation, and support/maintenance.

An example of the application of the model in education is agenda setting by a national or regional government that aims at making a population bilingual. Policy formulation will then consist of the development of primary and secondary school curricula. Policy implementation will include the provision of budgetary resources and the recruitment of

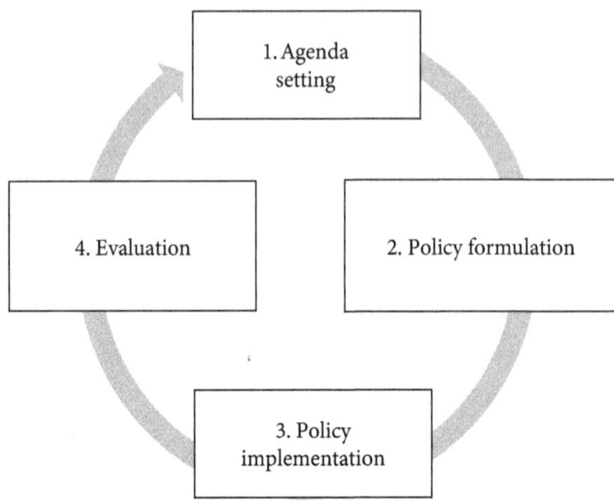

Figure 1 The Policy Cycle Model, after Climent-Ferrando (2023)

qualified teachers capable of providing an education that achieves the policy objectives. And evaluation includes regular reviews of the results and, if necessary, recommendations for improvement. Couched in a curriculum and a single institution, this idealized case seems manageable; however, as will become clear in subsequent chapters, in actual practice language policies are more complicated and more difficult to subject to the policy cycle model, which nevertheless offers a useful orientation to a policy field that is still evolving.

Further reading

Cooper, Robert L. 1996. *Language Planning and Social Change*. New York: Cambridge University Press.

Heller, Monica. 2018. Socioeconomic junctures, theoretical shifts: A genealogy of language policy and planning research. In James W. Tollefson, and Miguel Pérez-Milans (eds.), *The Oxford Handbook of Language Policy and Planning*, online edn., https://doi.org/10.1093/oxfordhb/9780190458898.013.6.

Shohamy, Elana. 2006. *Language Policy: Hidden Agendas and New Approaches*. London: Routledge.

2

Basic concepts and theories

> Indian Tamil man, 85, burns himself to death in Hindi language protest against government
>
> Farmer MV Thangavel doused himself in petrol and set himself alight, police say; he held a Tamil-language placard saying, 'Modi government, stop imposing Hindi'. AFP 27 November 2022
>
> Indian state administrations use regional languages, while the country's great linguistic diversity has favoured English as the language of communication between communities. Prime Minister Narendra Modi would prefer to see Hindi in this role.

To deal with language as a subject of political considerations, we need some tools. This chapter introduces a select number of concepts and briefly explains their theoretical relevance. The list is by no means complete; however, it opens a perspective on the link between language and politics. This link implies a view of language that differs from views characteristic of theoretical linguistics and other fields of language studies. The fact that there are various such views, not necessarily competing, is only to show that language is a complex phenomenon. Important for the present purposes is that nothing that can be subject of policy decisions is God-given or genetically inherited, although, as will become apparent in the chapters that follow, this is not always reflected in political discourse.

Language Policy. Florian Coulmas, Oxford University Press. © Florian Coulmas (2025).
DOI: 10.1093/9780191976377.003.0002

My purpose with the terms discussed in what follows is to chart out the territory in which language policy unfolds and to show that it is characterized by a multitude of decisions that can be contentious as they may confer advantages to some but not to others.

Politics

Politics is the exercise of power, a set of mechanisms of achieving societal goals by way of resolving differences in group interests. The term itself is derived from the Greek word *polis*, the city state inhabited, as mentioned in the previous chapter, by Aristotle's *zoon politicon*, the language-endowed political animal. *Polis* meant both government and society; however, in modern times, these spheres are held distinct, society, state, and government being dealt with by different branches of political science that investigate structural relationships between the individual and the community, group formation and interactions between groups, forms of steering human behaviour, and the state as an overarching construction of institutions designed to organize the political process, which can be depicted in terms of the policy cycle model introduced at the end of the previous chapter. On a comparative level, politics is concerned with the principles of government in different kinds of states, such as direct and representative democracies, parliamentary constitutional monarchies, absolute monarchies, theocracies, military dictatorships, and semi-autonomous territories. In all of these areas of politics language has a role to play that goes far beyond the default structure or epiphenomenon that some social scientists consider it to be. While it is true that language is always and inevitably related to the vicissitudes of society and politics, this does not make it a fixture, if only because there is a great variety of linguistic configurations in states and politically demarcated territories.

Politics is about choice. It is about who chooses what, why, and how, and about the organizational structures that regulate choices. These can be institutions that have the power to make laws and regulations, or set the goals for future development. Relations to other states, alliances, and international organizations are a matter of choice, as are ideologies embraced by groups of people and supported, tolerated, or banned by the state. The choice of means of social control has repercussions with regard to local, regional, national, and international concerns. Who is eligible to receive an education, to vote, to be elected to office, to establish a business, to get married, to post a text message, with what content? Or to speak their language in court, in a municipal assembly, in the classroom at school? These are political questions to which different political systems give different answers, all of which, however, pertain to power differentials. Politics with no relation to power is a contradiction in terms.

Politics can thus also be understood as the acting out of conflict, negotiation, and conciliation, in which state institutions and civil society actors such as pressure groups are involved, and, in the age of the digital economy where tech giants command budgets that are larger than those of some states, companies. The relative novelty of the IT industry and the fact that state regulation lags behind technological development reminds us of the fact that politics is contingent, always faced with new circumstances and challenges, which also implies that, unless they remain very abstract, definitions of what politics is change in step with changing times.

Diversity

Diversity is another concept that moves with the times. Derived from Latin *diversitas*, it has been present in the English language for centuries, but has only gained much prominence in the media as well as scholarly publications and in political discussions in recent decades. Industrial society in the framework of the national state played down variety and cultivated homogeneity, reflecting to some extent the constraints of mass-production where the desired uniformity of the manufactured goods necessitates a uniform production process. Diversity was not only undesirable; it was a deviation. The keywords for a well-functioning society were *adaptation*, *fitting*, and *assimilation*. Where heterogeneity was too conspicuous to overlook, the 'melting pot' was a metaphor that embodied a vision for the future. The nation state that aligns nation with language was seen as the most promising framework for establishing representative governance grounded in a shared public sphere where deliberation and mutual understanding are ensured by a shared language. The conditions for creating a unilingual state were never present in European colonies; nevertheless, the concept of a national language was often adopted as part of post-colonial nation building (see Chapter 5).

Diversity became a buzzword roughly at the same time when the dangers of emphasizing crop specialization in industrial agriculture became more widely recognized and led to a rethinking of how to balance the demands of efficiency and a healthy ecosystem. In this context, (bio-) diversity became something decidedly positive, an asset to be protected. As the notion migrated to other realms of thought, different kinds of diversity experienced a re-evaluation, too. Instead of equality in the spirit of the French Revolution, human rights activists began to stress the values of being different in human society where it is now used as a catchword to call people out against discrimination based on race, ethnicity, language, gender, sexual orientation, disability, religion, and other traits commonly referred to nowadays as 'identity' (Coulmas 2019; Fukuyama 2018; Griffiths 2021).

The diversity that matters most to LP is, of course, that of languages. It is therefore worth noting that the frequency of use of the term 'multilingualism' has increased over time exactly in parallel to that of 'diversity' (Figure 2).

Abstand and ausbau

The human species has produced a great many languages, which in general linguistics are all conceived of as expressions of the same underlying faculty of language. In the absence of objective criteria for distinguishing languages from dialects, counting languages is notoriously difficult. This is not much of a problem for linguistic theory, but for language policy it can be because it involves the questions of what counts as a language and what separates one from another. In order to come to grips with the problem, two terms that were coined by linguist Heinz

(a)

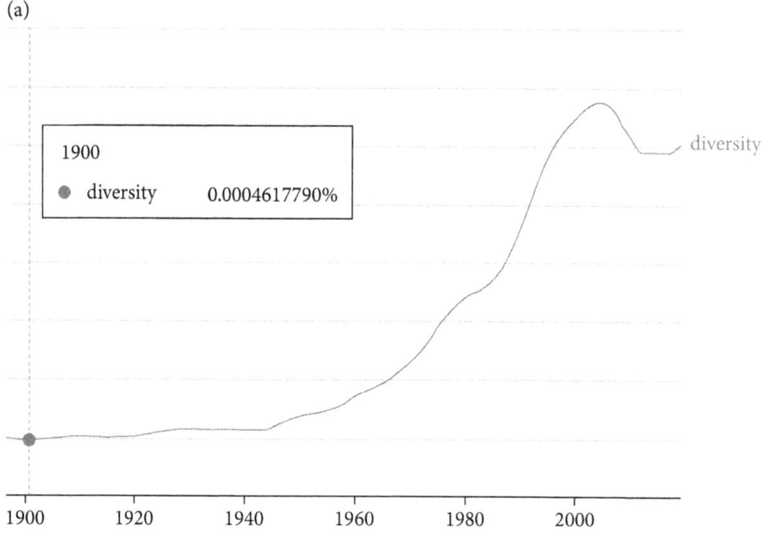

(b)

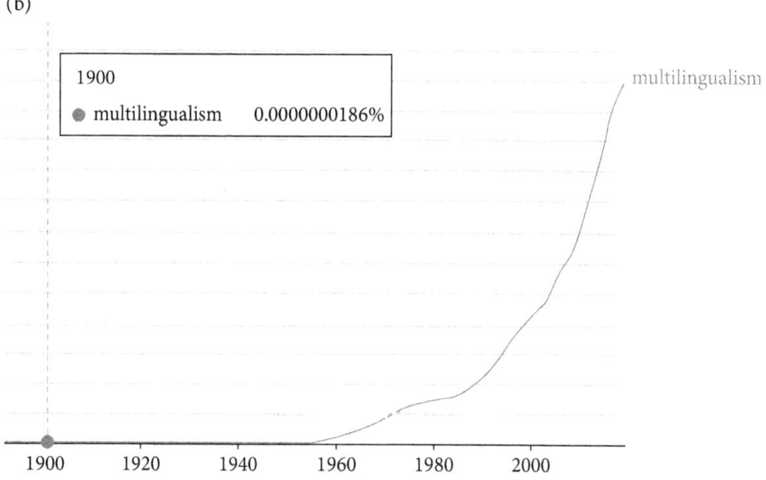

Figure 2 Frequency of occurrence of the terms *diversity* and *multilingualism* over the last century, as measured by Google Ngram Viewer

Kloss (1967) are widely used in language policy studies, '*abstand* language' and '*ausbau* language'. German *abstand* means 'distance' and is used to describe languages that have no close genealogical relations with each other. Think of English and Japanese. In terms of grammar, phonology, and lexicon these two languages are as different as can be and no one would ever suggest that one is related to or derived from the other. *Ausbau* means 'expansion' or 'elaboration' and is used to describe the relationship between languages that are different but closely related. Think of Croatian and Bosnian, Dutch and German, or Catalan and Spanish. These three pairs share over 80 per cent of their vocabulary, while the common lexical stock of Ukrainian and Russian amounts to some 62 per cent. In Russia, Ukrainian has long been called 'Little Russian' (*Malorossiya*), however, Ukrainian split off centuries ago to become an *ausbau* language—though still not recognized as such by many Russians, especially at times of war (Seals 2019). How low the percentage of shared vocabulary should be in order for coexisting varieties to be treated as two languages is still an open question which cannot be answered on the basis of cyphers alone. The two concepts of *abstand* language and *ausbau* language show how sensitive this question can be and offer some orientation on the rather confusing terrain of the world's languages, especially with regard to their status, which is of particular importance for LP purposes.

Status planning

The basic equality of all languages is an axiom of linguistic theory; in language policy it does not apply, for the differences between languages is its ultimate rationale. The status of a language in a polity is what, from a language policy point of view, distinguishes it from others. Conferring to a language a certain status can be and often is the result of a policy decision, as Haugen (1959) was among the first to discuss for Norway. A language has a status only in a certain environment and relative to other languages. Such an environment can be a state, a municipality, a community, an international organization, a company, or some other body whose members deem it expedient to determine the function and standing of one or several languages by law, decree, or holding on to tradition. Accordingly, status planning is one of the core fields of language policy, where decisions are taken to recognize a language as national, official, working, or minority language. The last-mentioned example points to the fact that declared status may create rather than reflect facts, as when some minority languages are recognized as such, but others not. Language policy thus intervenes in existing language regimes or status distributions (Hill 2010). How and whether status directed interventions succeed are research questions to be studied, for example by means of the policy cycle model mentioned above (p. 8).

Like other policy decisions, the attribution of language status can only be a declaration of intent, the implementation of which requires interventions at the level of the language itself, its 'corpus'.

Corpus planning

The second branch of language policy, corpus planning, is concerned with equipping languages with the means that are necessary to fulfil the functions associated with the status assigned to them. Standardization of grammar, providing a language with a writing system, orthography, or script, reforming existing writing systems, augmenting the lexicon to make a language suitable for purposes (e.g., higher education) it has not been used for before are corpus planning activities. As a conscious intervention in language development, corpus planning arose with the modern state where it played an important role for promoting linguistic unification or, in the contrary, separation. In both cases the purpose is to make a variety a language of power, which, as is commonly understood, can only be done in writing. Thus, by definition, corpus planning operates on a written norm or, in the absence of such, creates one. Corpus planning has been an important aspect of nation building, as in Europe a distinct language became increasingly seen as a criterion of political independence or nationhood and states, especially democratically organized ones, came to be conceptualized as requiring a proper national language to express themselves, their laws, and their policies. Maximizing the differences among nations can be a purpose of corpus planning (Wright 2015).

Acquisition planning

For corpus planning, as distinct from status planning, linguistic expertise is indispensable, but it is not enough to ensure the realization of overarching language policy goals, because language exists but in society. If a language has been chosen for certain functions, for example education, it must be equipped for the job and the community must be ready to accept it for that, which cannot be taken for granted. This is where acquisition planning, a term first introduced by educational psychologist Robert Cooper (1989), comes into play as a third language policy branch, which is sometimes augmented by 'prestige planning', for instance, when the popular image of a variety does not make it seem suitable for use at school. Institutionalizing a language as a language of instruction has far-reaching consequences for the relationship between speakers of different dialects and languages in the same polity (cf. Hogan-Brun, Robinson, and Thonhauser 2013). Sociologist Pierre Bourdieu (1991) introduced the notion of 'legitimate language' into the discourse about the relationships between language, state, and society, which captures the aspect of explicit and implicit claims on the part of the government and its representatives regarding language varieties and usage. Languages prioritized by the state gain prestige that others do not and have an influence on access to rewarding workplaces which may, therefore, meet with resistance by (parts of) the population or by teachers who feel the value of their qualifications threatened. These are just some of the social configurations that have to be considered to ensure the successful realization of language policy goals. Aside from official language policies, individual households may decide on their own rules of language use. Migrants, for example, often make a deliberate choice to use their heritage language at home in order to enable smooth communication between grandchildren raised in the destination country and grandparents left behind by their migrant children (e.g., Liu 2018). Conversely, using the destination country's dominant language at home in the interest of quick integration can also be a deliberate choice.

There are, moreover, many language groups, both 'territorial' minorities who have lived in a state territory for a long time, and migrants that enjoy no official support. For them, acquisition planning becomes a matter of what has been called 'family language policy' (King, Fogle, and Logan-Terry 2008), which comprises language practices within the family based on guiding beliefs and ideologies.

Domain

State-run schools and education generally are important fields of activity for language policy or *domains*, to use a term introduced by sociolinguist Joshua Fishman (1972) who distinguished five domains of language use, namely family, friendship, religion, education, and work. The concept of language domains directs our attention to the fact that within a society a language is used in one place and with a particular group of interlocutors, but not with others; in other words, that the monolingual speaker and the monolingual society are just one model among others. In fact, the domain-specific use of languages, dialects, and other varieties is far more common, if not the default case. In some cases this is regulated by rules of procedure or even law; in others it is a matter of convention and tradition. Many modern constitutions contain provisions on language, designating one or more languages as official or national. In what language(s) bills are drafted, deliberated in the legislature, and enacted as laws is regulated. The state and its institutions constitute a sphere in which language choice is not left to the discretion of speakers acting in it.

Other domains typically distinguished include home and family, the market, military, politics (domestic and international), and science. Cultural activities, the media, and the public sphere including social media in cyberspace could be added. Online communication is particularly important, because, as is usually the case when societies and legal codes are confronted with major technological innovations, legal regulation lags behind (Shandilya and Kumari 2022). Language policy in these domains has repercussions for pupils' educational attainment, social stratification, participation, inclusion, and exclusion, and in this sense for democracy. Opening up a domain for a language, for instance by bilingual education legislation, and expanding a language into a new domain by means of officially supported corpus planning, are LP goals that can impact the course of a society's development, as examples will demonstrate in subsequent chapters.

Proficiency

Fluent command of a language is hard to assess and relative by nature, since what for one purpose may count as fluent may be insufficient for another. Accordingly, various proficiency scales have been proposed.[1] For technical purposes language proficiency is often defined circularly as the ability to pass a proficiency test. As physical labour has increasingly been replaced by communication and information processing, exams of this sort have gained importance in recent decades, in immigration contexts, education, business, and the military. Standards, usually for the four basic skills—speaking and listening, reading and writing—in the dominant language, are set for specific purposes related to work, studying at a university, entry visas, permanent residence or citizenship. Minimum levels of test results, while not arbitrary, are subjective, purpose specific, and adjustable by political decisions.

Language shift

Decreasing proficiency in a language can also be observed independently of formal test settings, paradigmatically in immigrant groups who do not transmit their language to the subsequent generation, either due to political pressure to assimilate from the receiving state or motivated by cost-benefit considerations that make the forebears' language seem economically worthless. In both cases the speech community undergoes language shift from their language of origin to the dominant language of their new home country. Because this does not happen overnight and groups differ with regard to how long—for how many generations—they maintain their heritage language, language shift is a standard topic of sociolinguistics, and since policies of the recipient state may steer this process in one way or another, it is a subject of LP which in recent decades also confronts the fate of numerically small Indigenous languages (Austin and Sallabank 2011).

Endangered language

Language shift in migrant communities usually has little or no effect on the language as spoken in their country of origin; however, language shift is not limited to migrants. As one of the consequences of the transformative role of the state in the wake of industrialization and the globalization process of the present age, ever fewer small-scale population groups with their own culture and language live in isolation. Being increasingly integrated into national communities, many of these groups abandon their language in favour of the country's dominant language. In the 1980s, this kind of language shift came to be viewed as an undesirable development that gave rise to the term 'endangered language', evidently inspired by the ecological notion of endangered species (Sutherland 2003). As it suggests a political responsibility to halt or reverse the trend, it is relevant to language policy, as will be discussed in more detail in Chapter 10.

The idea of language endangerment is deeply embedded in postmodern and decolonization ideology which, as distinct from modernization ideology, values plurality in society and language as well as individual and group rights regardless of whether they enhance or conflict with national goals.

Language rights

For a long time, the legal aspects of language use in a polity were implicit. The formation of national states produced many 'minority languages' that in most cases were subjected to government directives or just ignored. The ideas that languages deserve to be protected on the part of the state and that individuals or groups—another contentious question: can groups claim and be accorded rights?—have the right to use their language are still quite new. As of the

1990s, individual choice of language use has been frequently framed in scholarly and political debates as a human rights issue which protects individual freedom while allowing a language to flourish (Chen 1998; Patten and Kymlicka 2003; Skutnabb-Kangas and Phillipson 2023). The consequences of including choice and use of language in civil rights for the state is a matter of debate on many language policy agendas nowadays, where whether a distinction should be made between migrants' languages and languages of autochthonous ethnicities is one of the issues. Whether language use serves instrumental functions, i.e., communicating contents, or symbolic functions, i.e., marking group affiliation and valuation of a tradition, are two additional aspects of this debate that are equally important and not always easy to separate.

Language planning

Implementing language policies is generally called 'language planning'. Language policy defines political goals that are then to be realized through language planning using concrete plans and strategies, for example plans for an official language rights regime for a state, its institutions, and its citizens. The policy cycle model can once again be adduced here as an analytic tool, for language planning involves goal-oriented measures to influence both speakers' language behaviour and language, that is, a community language, its corpus as defined above. An alternative concept that is used to systematize the decision-making processes of language planning is 'language management', first promoted by linguists Björn H. Jernudd and Jiří V. Neustupný (1987). Language management is intended to solve language problems in a society. It operates on individual and collective levels ranging from guidelines for individual utterances—e.g., news anchor pronunciation and terminology rules—to the diffusion of linguistic standards in education, decisions about foreign language instruction, and international language-spread policies.

Conceptualizing language as an object of planning or management is not a matter of course, especially not for those who, taking up attitudes to language first formulated in the context of nineteenth-century

Romanticism, see languages as natural growths and accordingly conceive of linguistic diversity in analogy to biodiversity. There is a certain tension between management and planning which applies to artefacts, on the one hand, and natural organisms which thrive or are superseded by others that are better adjusted to the environment, on the other. Hard empirical evidence of the benefits of preserving languages is hard to come by. In the absence of such, the analogy of linguistic and natural diversity could simply be understood as an appeal to support endangered languages by evoking the need to protect the environment against human destruction, which by now is widely recognized as important in many countries. Although the reasons may be obscure or yet unknown to us, the multiplicity of languages is seen as a common good worth preserving for posterity,[2] which given the homogenizing forces of global capitalist expansion requires human intervention.

Language ideology

Diversity is good. Homogeneity is good. Bilingualism is bad for cognitive development. Our language is better than yours. As a proper nation we need a national language. The masculine generic cements asymmetric relationships between the sexes in society. Foreign words corrupt our language. These are beliefs grounded in language ideologies. The challenge for the scientific study of language policy is to analyse such ideologies without being (too much) committed to one of them. The caveat in brackets is in order because social sciences, even if they try to reduce everything to empirically verifiable theories, are never free of subjectivity and the researcher's point of view.

Looking at the language situation of a society from the outside, in the sense that the researcher is not connected to it by any personal relationships or interests, can be helpful, but also bears the risk of missing important aspects of the language policy problems at hand. For example, from a structural and lexicographical perspective, language differentiation can seem like a triviality when two varieties are very similar and largely intercommunicable, such as Afrikaans and Dutch; but linguistic nationalism, authenticity, independence, and other ideologemes may make differentiation very important for one or both parties and would thus influence design and implementation of language policy. Who should decide? Who has linguistic authority? This is another question that has little if any significance for language conceived as an abstract system, but is of great importance when looked at as communicative practice; for here language ideology comes into play. It relates to ideas about the nature of language. Is language a natural organism or is it a communication tool that we have shaped and continually adapt to exigencies? Such beliefs, as is often the case with ideologically tinted views, may not be held consciously but uncritically taken for granted as implicit socially accepted knowledge. Whether, how, and by whom a language can be regulated and politically instrumentalized will to some extent depend on such views.

Ideological conceptions of the nature of language can be harmless. Things are different when they are morally loaded and combined with discriminatory motivations that impact communicative practices in shaping social structures. Purism is a case in point. It appears to refer to language only and provides the justification to fight foreign infiltration and the denaturation of the native language, which embodies one's culture and heritage. However, there is plenty of evidence that the purist drive to eliminate undesirable loanwords is intertwined with xenophobia and nationalism. Against this backdrop, the question arises how an ideologically shaped communicative practice will impact social conduct.

Language ideologies are embedded in broader intellectual currents, as attested, for example, by the changing assessment of homogeneity and diversity. In the twenty-first century, diversity along various parameters including language is valued more in many places than it was in the twentieth. Accordingly, multilingualism has a better name now than it had in the past, a 'change of mind' which may very well influence research on communicative practices.

Thus, language ideologies are of interest on two planes. One is the formation and implementation of language policy and the other research about it (see Blommaert 1999; Woolard 2020 for examples). This should be kept in mind when considering the public role of language policy research, for example when academics serve as policy advisers, engage in public debates about language issues, support particular interest groups, etc. Their views are perspectival inevitably reflecting an ideological standpoint.

Theory or theories

The concepts discussed above cover a wide range of language policy issues. Different as they are in contents, they share the characteristics of many social science concepts, contingency and fuzziness. Many are volatile, changing their meaning with time, context, and the agents using them. What does this imply for theory? How scientific is the scholarly field of language policy? Are there any schemes for relating methods to goals, and for empirically testing the applied methods' effectiveness? The answer is, not much beyond the policy cycle model, for we are dealing with individuals and groups who cannot easily be subjected to experiments.[3] Evidence-based studies of LP effectiveness such as Terasawa (2018) are still few and far between, and this study is limited to assessing the effectiveness of English language teaching as an LP goal. Further, the two-faced nature of language as communicative tool and symbolic expression makes it impossible to develop research designs and reduce all findings to dry statistics while ignoring human passion and strive. There are theories, but not a general theory of language policy.

Above all, what is needed is a general theory to explain the circumstances that provoke conflict between language communities and how such conflicts can be avoided. To date, such a theory does not exist. It does not exist because, rather than being an isolated matter, language policy is always interwoven with other social, economic, and cultural phenomena.

Existing theories are to do with decision making, with group formation, boundaries (political and linguistic), psychological attitudes, language contact, language cultivation (corpus planning), among others. Within the framework of these various theories, hypotheses are formulated which can be tested, if not experimentally, then by comparing data from different national, regional, municipal, and institutional contexts. Historical comparisons are also often instructive. Consider the following hypotheses:

Efficiency beats beauty: language choices are mostly based on speakers' cost-benefit tallying.
Democracy requires unilingualism.
Linguistic pluralism is detrimental to economic development.
For nationalism to be fostered, a national language is indispensable.
Repressing minority languages will mitigate ethnic tensions.
Repressing minority languages will reinforce ethnic tensions.
With regard to language rights, there is a fundamental difference between autochthonous and migrant minorities.
A national public sphere that offers all members of society the ability to participate cannot exist with internal language divisions.

The merits of these and other hypotheses can be tested by studying individual cases or assembling data across polities whereby the difficulties of obtaining an objective standpoint must not be forgotten. Reflecting for example on the last-mentioned hypothesis, the 'public sphere' is a notion that was introduced in sociological theory to explain certain aspects of modernity and early democracy. That 'public sphere' today, under communication conditions that were unimaginable two centuries ago and even in the 1960s when the theory of the public sphere was first floated, still means what it meant then is anything but self-evident. This has been acknowledged by social philosopher Jürgen Habermas (1991) who was the most influential theoretician of the public sphere in the 1980s. Recognizing the social impact of the digital turn he speaks of a 'new structural transformation of the public sphere' (Coulmas 2023; Habermas 2022; also below 141f.). Nationalism is another historically conditioned notion. Although in other parts of the world the European idea of 'one language, one territory, one nation' served as a template, its practical significance in post-colonial countries is different, not least because of the legacy of the colonial languages (Makoni, Severo, and Abdelhay 2023). The multitude of languages within state borders manifests itself in many different configurations and affects nation-building processes, the stability of states or, in the contrary, their disintegration in various ways.

Language is a rule-governed system. Without rules, communication would be impossible. Society is an ordered community of people. Without order, social life would be impossible. Since language rules and social ordering principles are not congruent, there is plenty of room for, and often a need of language policy action. It is the multiplicity of interrelations between language, polity, and politics that will be fathomed below by means of the concepts introduced in this chapter and their application in different countries and with regard to language problems that call for a political solution.

In trying to understand the complexities of developing social situations involving language and politics, ideological competition, historical experience, and generational differences also require our attention.

Further reading

Cooper, Robert L. 1989. *Language Planning and Social Change*. Cambridge: Cambridge University Press.

Coulmas, Florian. 2019. *Identity. A Very Short Introduction*. Oxford: Oxford University Press.

Kloss, Heinz. 1967. *Abstand* languages and *Ausbau* languages. *Anthropological Linguistics* 9: 29–41.

Wright, Sue. 2004. *Language Policy and Language Planning: From Nationalism to Globalisation*. Basingstoke: Palgrave.

3

Language conflicts

> What's a language? "Contemporary **B**osnian, **C**roatian, and **S**erbian are spoken by about 17 million people and are nearly identical to each other in vocabulary and grammar, though they use different alphabets. Depending on one's point of view, then, studying BCS offers three languages and two alphabets for the price of one course." Department of Slavic Languages & Literatures, Harvard University.[1]
>
> When Yugoslavia disintegrated and war broke out in the 1990s, 'Serbo-Croatian' also broke up and was fragmented into Serbian, Croatian, and Bosnian. The Dayton Peace Agreement of 1995 was written and signed in all three languages.

When communication between monarchs and subjects is limited to tax collection and, perhaps, call-up to military service, as in pre-modern European kingdoms and empires, language is not much of an issue. With the fragmentation of states in the course of modernization, it became one of increasing urgency. The establishment of national states as principal units of the world order in the nineteenth and twentieth centuries co-occurred with a fundamental restructuring of communication between ruler and ruled. After the French Revolution, democratization and the emergence of the nation state as the dominant principle of political organization progressed hand in hand, encouraging and necessitating more intense communication among citizens and between people and government. Because of the great number of languages and dialects, this necessity was not easily met, and still isn't in many parts of the world.

Language Policy. Florian Coulmas, Oxford University Press. © Florian Coulmas (2025).
DOI: 10.1093/9780191976377.003.0003

Max Weber (1968) matter-of-factly described his time around the turn of the twentieth century as the 'age of language conflicts'. The principal reason for that, he explained, was that 'nation state' had become conceptually identical with 'state' based on a common language and the rise of nationalism. That was a century ago. Where do we stand today?

In the course of the last one hundred years, this characterization has become if anything more cogent. In a world divided into some 200 polities whose inhabitants speak some 7000 languages, controversies about language(s) and state authority over language are, if not the only, very important reasons for the existence of language policy as a field of government action at different levels. That it rose to prominence in Weber's lifetime had much to do with the rise of nationalism. Prioritizing one language over others in a polity will be shown in this chapter to have played a significant role in modern nation building. As Weber also observed, referring to the Irish, the Swiss and the German-speaking Alsatians, a shared language facilitates communication within a group, but is not always sufficient to constitute a communal relationship, or necessary to sustain a sense of national identity. For in addition to proclaimed monolingual nation states there are many others that comprise several language groups.[2]

This chapter concentrates on policy questions revolving around this relationship and its implications for access to power and political participation in democratic and authoritarian regimes. It pays particular attention to language policy issues in Belgium, Canada, the United States, Pakistan, and Yugoslavia and its successor states.

Belgium

The Kingdom of Belgium is regionally divided into Dutch-speaking Flanders bordering the Netherlands to the north, French-speaking Wallonia bordering France to the south, some German-speaking communities near the German border to the east, and the officially French-Dutch bilingual Brussels-Capital Region. After the separation of the southern provinces from the Netherlands in the wake of the Napoleonic Wars and the establishment of Belgium as a sovereign state in 1830–31, language-centred conflicts between the francophone and Flemish-speaking Belgians were high on the political agenda of the new state. Initially, this coincided with tensions between the ruling elite, who preferred to speak French, and the Flemish, who felt their language underrepresented in state institutions. At the national level, French was the only official language of the country until 1898. This status discrepancy with Flemish contributed much to politicizing the latter. Several constitutional amendments and the gradual democratization of the country addressed the French-Flemish chasm, but for a long time did little to defuse the conflict potential. Time and again governments were brought down by language disputes they were unable to resolve.

As a consequence, linguistic divisions related to historical and economic differences between Wallonia and Flanders have shaped Belgian politics more than anything else. An array of laws and language management measures from the national to local levels still have not eliminated the risk of political deadlock. In 2010, negotiations by French and Dutch-speaking politicians over redrawing the boundaries of the bilingual voting district Brussels Halle-Vilvoorde broke down, forcing premier Yves Leterme to resign—nothing new for Belgians, who have seldom seen a government remain in office for the entire legislature, despite the many regulations that secure parity of the two main language communities. To them, this is a familiar story that has actually been subjected to a 'storytelling analysis' (De Keere and Elchardus 2011). Such an approach is very suitable for understanding the motivations and dynamics of this conflict, since people have opinions and tell their own stories about it.

Today, the Belgian Constitution, in its most recent version of March 2021,[3] is hailed as a carefully designed, detailed, and easily accessible legislation with regard to languages that has few competitors; 34 of its 198 articles comprise some 200 sections with provisions on language. The result of decades of negotiations between the two main language groups, the legislation is extremely comprehensive, but still not foolproof against unforeseen language policy problems, real or made-up.

As laid down in its Article 189, 'constitutional texts are established in French, in Dutch, and in German' and consequently have the same legal force in these three languages. By and large, language provisions in Belgium are based on the territoriality principle that gives preference to one language in a designated area that is officially recognized notably for use in schools, public administrations, and courtrooms. This can, however, be tricky because historically residence patterns did not evolve according to deliberate designs that separate language communities from each other, as the above-mentioned bilingual voting district of Brussels Halle-Vilvoorde illustrates.

Constitutional amendments in the course of the past one hundred years were characterized by a tendency towards political decentralization shifting responsibilities for language matters increasingly from the national to regional and community legislations and administrations. The general purpose of language-related legislation is to prevent conflicts and, where this turns out to be impossible, to make them manageable. Some of the provisions are, accordingly, very specific, as for example Art. 4 (3) which is concerned with Belgium's four linguistic regions:

> The limits of the four linguistic regions can only be changed or modified by a law adopted by majority vote in each linguistic group in each House, on the condition that the majority of the members of each group are gathered together and from the moment that the total of affirmative votes given by the two linguistic groups is equal to at least two thirds of the votes expressed.

Another provision stipulates that draft bills in the national parliament must be suspended when at least three quarters of one linguistic group declare that it would gravely damage relations between the linguistic communities (Art. 54 (1, 2)). And Art. 99 (2) requires that the Council of Ministers, the national government, includes as many French-speaking members as Dutch-speaking members.

Further, several provisions deal with the composition and the functioning of the three Councils, i.e., the French Community Council, the Flemish Community Council, and the German-speaking Community Council (Art. 118).

Seemingly unbridgeable differences about language policy and the resultant regionalization have called the very existence of the state into question more than once, but Belgium's legislators have worked hard to build a functioning language regime; yet the legislation that establishes the language rights of the citizenry according to designated territories is not a definitive solution of language conflicts. The far-reaching transfer of language policy authority from the national government to the regions cannot inhibit the ongoing demographic changes. This is most noticeable in Brussels. In the officially bilingual Capital Region international English has gained a noticeable presence as the dominant language of European institutions whose position is further strengthened by the pressures of globalization and migration. At the turn of the century, 10.1 per cent of Brussels' inhabitants came from Wallonia, 8.4 per cent from Flanders, and 31.7 per cent were born abroad. By 2023, the foreign-born population was approaching 70 per cent, 32.1 per cent hailing from European countries and 36 per cent from outside Europe, many of whom form ethnic communities that speak their own languages and have little competence in either of the two official languages of the region. Migration flows are the largest influence on the region's population composition, making it increasingly difficult to uphold the bilingual language regime according to which school education and public services are only offered in French and Dutch. Increasing population diversity poses new challenges.

Still, Belgium, having weathered many language conflicts, has valuable language policy lessons to teach to plurinational, multilingual democracies. It is no coincidence that a pioneer of language conflict studies was Belgian linguist Peter Nelde (cf. Darquennes 2015; Schiffman 2011).

One more aspect worth mentioning is to do with the potentially conflictual relationship between Flemish and Dutch. Increasing diversity characterizes not just Brussels, but Flanders as well where new immigrants arrive every day. Many of them do not speak the local language, which is one of the reasons for the Flemish civic integration programme that also includes language courses. The 'legitimate language' of these courses is standard Dutch, and the language pupils are taught in the elementary schools of Flanders is likewise standard Dutch. Since Flemish is a distinctly different variant of Dutch and Flanders split away from the rest of the Netherlands, the cultivation of Flemish as an ausbau language in its own right could have served as a means of promoting Flemish autonomy. This did not happen. Instead of pushing for linguistic independence the Flemish maintained, even strengthened, their links with Dutch. The Netherlands and Flanders cooperated in the field of Dutch LP and, in 1980, founded the *Taalunie*, Union for the Dutch Language,[4] an organization designed to cultivate and promote Dutch in the Netherlands, Flanders, Suriname, and other Dutch-speaking territories. A complex situation like this one has given rise to the question whether a language policy organization such as the *Taalunie* needs to develop a language-variation policy, which Bennis and Blom affirm. Such a policy, they recommend, should be based on two principles.

(1) There are no good or bad varieties of Dutch but only varieties that are more or less appropriate in specific contexts.
(2) Good knowledge of the standard language is a prerequisite for full participation in our societies (Bennis and Blom 2019: 144).

Distinguishing their language from Dutch would have further weakened the Flemish's position in the linguistic hierarchy of Belgium. There the status rivalry with French, whose Belgian speakers have always claimed primacy for their language, was more important. This is a vivid example of the political dimension of language conflicts and the contingent factors affecting claims to language status.

Canada

French and English came to North America as the languages of major European powers and as such in time both would become what some called 'world languages'. Yet in the vast territory of British colonies first and then the Canadian Federation, officially proclaimed in 1867, a hierarchy developed between the two that gave rise to many conflicts, at times even threatening the unity of the state.

As early as 1841, the Act of Union had recognized English unilingualism in the provincial legislature of Canada, and in the second half of the nineteenth and early decades of the twentieth century, Canada's economic modernization and the spread of English across the continent set French speakers and the policies supporting them under severe pressure. In addition, still under British rule, there were policies at provincial and regional levels that actively repressed the use of French, such as the cancellation of official bilingualism in Manitoba in 1890 and the restriction of French language instruction in Ontario schools in 1913. The 'Conscription Crisis' of 1917 shook the very foundation of the Canadian polity, as the francophones were deeply opposed to being drafted into what they perceived as an English Canadian military at the service of the British Empire. The crisis did not end with the end of the war; the memory of it served as a lasting reinforcement of the linguistic divide. These and other occurrences bolstered the linguistic hierarchy with English at the top and French second. It would still take many decades before other languages—Indigenous languages, by natives, and heritage languages, by migrants—would enter the picture (Weinstein 1983: 143f.; Brook 2024).

In the meantime, English was emerging as the language of commerce across North America, which only served further to diminish the strength and appeal of French. The increasing inequality between anglophone and francophone Canadians translated into growing economic disparity (Nadeau 2009). Language policy often has an economic dimension in the sense that one language is found to be economically more valuable than another by both its native and second language speakers. In Canada this has been very noticeable, which is of interest since the difference was not between a European power language and a local language of a small community but between two European imperial languages that ranked equally in Europe and other parts of the world.

French Canadians continued to assert the vitality and importance of their language in public and private life, but due to increasing economic inequality between anglophones and francophones the linguistic divide developed into a threat to the Canadian state, as francophone nationalists began to call not only for the protection of the French language but for Quebec's separation from Canada. The Canadian government responded to this challenge in the 1960s by setting up the Royal Commission on Bilingualism and Biculturalism. The commission's findings led to the Official Languages Act,[5] passed by the Canadian parliament in 1969 in a spirit of 'equal partnership' of English and French.

The Official Languages Act was repeatedly updated, last in 2023, when the House of Commons passed Bill C-13[6], *An Act for the Substantive Equality of Canada's Official Languages.* It originally stipulated that all official language versions of this and other acts are equally authoritative and comprises provisions for legislative rules and regulations, the administration of justice, services to and communication with the public, language of work, equal opportunity of employment in federal institutions, and a general commitment to the advancement of English and French in Canada. Because Canadian federalism allows provinces to formulate their own language policies there are differences between the provinces. Most conspicuously, as the only French-majority province Quebec maintains official bilingualism at the federal level, but allows only French for use in its provincial institutions.

When Pierre Trudeau, prime minister from 1968 to 1979 and from 1980 to 1984, introduced the Official Languages Bill to parliament he made a distinction between dualism and bilingualism, arguing that the former was divisive giving rise to two separate governments, while the latter embodied the strength of 'a country which had learned to speak in two great languages'.[7] In this sense the act must be seen as promoting bilingualism while countering separatism (of Quebec). The overarching language policy guarantees citizens the right to use their language of choice in various domains. Since this is conditional on factors such as sufficient public demand to use French in an English-majority environment or vice versa, it is an approach that fused the territoriality principle and the personality principle, i.e., the idea that every individual should enjoy the right to speak their language. For the same reason, there are still provisions that are contested, as the various laws and policies governing language rights are not always consistent.

Bill C-13 was designed to bring the Official Language Act up to date. By strengthening the rights for French-speaking communities across the country the legislature hoped to come closer to realizing the purpose of the Official Language Act which is 'to ensure respect for English and French as the official languages of Canada, to support and encourage their development in linguistic minority communities and generally to promote their equal status and use in Canadian society' (Bourgeois 2023). Bill C-13 did bring about a substantial change to the Official Language Act which was welcomed by many. However, since demographic dynamics continue, the need for further amendments is only a matter of time.

For instance, section 23 of the Charter of Rights and Freedoms guarantees minority language education rights to French-speaking communities outside Quebec, and to English-speaking minorities in Quebec.

Canadian citizens living outside of Quebec have the right to send their children to French schools if:

- their mother tongue is French;
- they attended French primary and secondary schools in Canada;
- they have a child who has attended or is attending French primary or secondary schools in Canada.

Canadian citizens living in Quebec have the right to send their children to English schools if:

- they themselves attended English primary and secondary schools in Canada;
- they have a child who has attended or is attending English primary or secondary schools in Canada.[8]

These rights are guaranteed 'where numbers warrant'. It has been argued that this caveat means that there is no freedom of choice for schooling in French outside Quebec; for where there is not a large enough number of people to justify applying this right, it is often the result of parents' poor schooling or the repression of French in the past and therefore only falsely suggests freedom of choice. New bills and regulations are for the future, but they inevitably carry a history with them that may reawaken past conflicts. In this case, the focus was on stemming the decline of French outside Quebec, but the means to do so proved inadequate. Bill C-13 was intended to correct this.

As for other language groups, particularly Indigenous minorities, they were too weak to pose a threat to political unity and were therefore repressed or ignored. This began to change only in the 1980s when the protection of ethnic and linguistic minorities gained some traction in the Western world. The Constitution Act of 1982 guaranteed the existing rights of Indigenous peoples and the Canadian Multiculturalism Act of 1987 made multiculturalism a policy goal. It found expression, among others, in the establishment of the Heritage Language Institute. At present it is part of the Indigenous Languages and Cultures Program of the Department of Canadian Heritage,[9] which coordinates and supports the efforts of Indigenous (First Nations, Inuit and Métis) communities and organizations to reclaim, revitalize, maintain, and strengthen Indigenous languages.

The Multiculturalism Act was an important step in the evolution of Canadian language policy which for a long time ignored the needs of francophones and all other communities that were unable to resist the steamrolling of English. This evolution encompassed a change of perspective from a purely utilitarian view of the instrumental functions of language to one that also recognizes its expressive functions for community formation and affiliation. Rather than limiting LP to designating one language, English, first and later two, English and French, as official for schooling and public administration while leaving culture, heritage, and minority languages to individuals and the groups concerned, it came to encompass state responsibility for the fate of Indigenous languages. The Statement of Reconciliation issued by the Canadian government in 1998 that openly addressed abuse at residential schools where Indigenous children were separated from their families was another policy act with the same intent. Change the past it cannot, but to some extent it can assist those who want to change the consequences of past repression, discrimination, and dispossession, including that of languages. The Indigenous Languages Act, which supports the revitalization, maintaining, and strengthening of Indigenous languages, was passed in 2019. Whether government sponsored language revitalization programmes will be successful is hard to predict, but the legislative recognition of Indigenous languages has fundamentally changed community relations between the majority society and its minorities, just as the Commission on Bilingualism and Biculturalism of the 1960s changed the relationship between francophone and anglophone Canadians. Not that all potential causes of frictions between language communities have been eliminated for good, but overall, the metamorphosis of Canadian language policy over the past half century contributed greatly to conflict reduction. Yet, language remains on the political agenda. In May 2022, Québec's National Assembly adopted Bill 96 designed to reform the charter of the French language and further strengthen the status of French by making it obligatory to use only French for official writing and speech. In the event, anglophone Quebecers took to the street to protest the law, effectively reversing, as it were, the conditions that for many decades had characterized anglophone-francophone relations across Canada. 'We are Quebecers, too', read one of their posters,[10] testifying to the enduring relevance of LP in Canadian politics.

Nowadays, the Canadian and Belgian language policies embody the zeitgeist that calls for a positive evaluation of diversity, and, if they have not falsified the hypothesis of nineteenth-century linguistic nationalism that a modern state can function only in a unilingual mode, they have certainly relativized it. A point of interest about these two cases is that the linguistic balance of power was opposite: in Belgium, French has been dominant since the founding of the state; in Canada it has always been subordinate, a good illustration of the fact that the political position of a language has less to do with its properties than it does with those who use it. Language issues still have not disappeared from everyday politics, but nowadays both states operate quite efficiently, which allows these countries to be among the richest in the world in terms of GDP per capita. In some cases, however, national wealth is a major factor of new language conflicts by attracting immigrants. The United States is a prime example.

United States

During his 2016 US presidential campaign, Donald Trump often said that 'in the United States you have to speak English' (Díez 2019), a paradigm example of language policy on the ground that everyone understood as being directed against Spanish and the continuing influx of immigrants from Latin American countries. While xenophobia and racism have often been the tacit reasons for advocating the adoption of English as an official language at all levels of government of the US, Trump's crude rhetoric opened the door a little wider for anti-Latino hate speech on social media (Lopez 2019). That 'in the US you have to speak English' is an opinion which, however, has no legal foundation. In the course of time, 32 US states have declared English the official language of the state, but there never was and still is no official language at the national level.[11]

Promoting English as the only national language of the United States is not a new idea. It flared up every now and then through history, gained some strength in the early twentieth century and in 1983 was given the label 'US English' by Samuel I. Hayakawa, a professor of English at San Francisco State University and then US Senator. Other movements with different names, such as 'English Only', but similar messages followed (Crawford 2000). Supported by many on the right side of the political spectrum. These initiatives met with harsh criticism on the left (e.g., Leibowicz 1984; Pullum 1991), where they were seen as incompatible with the pluralism and tolerance of a country of immigration and the right to free speech.

The officialization of English has often become an issue at election times and continues to do so to this day. Republican Congressmen have made it their task to convince Congress that English must be made the official language of the nation, repeatedly tabling bills to that effect.

As the Hispanic population keeps growing it is unlikely that this will change. In 2021 the US Hispanic population reached 62.5 million, an increase of 12 million since 2010, turning the Hispanics into the largest racial or ethnic group in some states, notably California and Texas (Krogstad, Passel and Noe-Bustamante 2022). In Texas, Hispanic students make up the majority of public-school students (Ura 2023). At close to half of its population New Mexico has been the most Latino state for some time. In several American cities the Hispanic population would make up large metropolises in their own right: New York City 2.4 million, Los Angeles 1.9 million, Chicago 773,000.

In view of the demographic developments exemplarily depicted in Table 1, eradicating languages other than English is no option, or no longer an option, one should say, recalling the long tradition of supressing Indigenous languages by locking their speakers' children up in English-medium boarding schools (Newland 2022). Today, Spanish is the most populous non-English language but, needless to say, there are many others. The data cited above is largely based on self-identification and does not reveal much about actual language proficiency in either Spanish or English, but the close association of language with ethnic identity and the sheer size of the Hispanic population inevitably make language a political issue, especially of language education policy, but not only. There is a social aspect to it, too, which becomes apparent, for example, when we know that the percentage of children growing up in low-income households is significantly higher for dual-language learner children than among children whose only home language is English (NALEO Educational Fund 2020).

Table 1 Percentage of Hispanics/Latinos in select US states

US State	Share of Hispanic population, 2021
New Mexico	50%
California	40%
Texas	40%
Arizona	32%
Florida	27%
New York	18%

Source: US Census Bureau, Krogstad, Passel, and Noe-Bustamante 2022

In view of the social dimensions of bilingualism and as an expression of the positive aspects of diversity that have gained ground in the age of identity, bilingual education programmes have been established in many schools across the US. New York, for example, has recognized students' home language as an 'an untapped resource' deserving to put to use for the benefit of the speakers and society at large.[12] Bilingual education programmes have been established in other states, too. They are not focussed on Spanish only and comprise many other languages, notably Indigenous languages (Crawley 2020). In 2021, the Biden White House launched a support initiative for American Indians and Alaska Natives which included a commitment to educational equity for native children.[13] However, no other language comes close to Spanish in population size and is, therefore, remotely as politically sensitive. In the event, the LP agenda in US states is driven largely by migration from Spanish-speaking countries. While migration has an impact on language policy in many places, history may be just as weighty a factor, as our next example shows.

Yugoslavia

The Socialist Federal Republic of Yugoslavia (SFR) was a state with a short history. Erected in the Balkans on the ruins of the Kingdom of Yugoslavia that existed from 1918 until 1941, the SFR of Yugoslavia lasted from 1945 until 1992 when it fell apart into the six republics of Slovenia, Serbia, Montenegro, Macedonia (later to be called Northern Macedonia), Croatia, and Bosnia and Herzegovina. It is not for nothing that *Balkanization* became an accepted term for fragmentation into conflict-prone polities. How many of them are there, and what is the role of language in this confusion? The title of Kamusella, Nomachi and Gibson's 2015 book suggests a multidimensional answer: *Handbook of Slavic Languages, Identities and Borders*. Conventionally six *Yugo*slavian or South Slavic—*yugo* means 'south'—languages are distinguished: Slovene, Serbian, Croatian, Bosnian, Macedonian, and Bulgarian have been described as one language with two scripts, as a dialect continuum, or as closely related South Slavic varieties of a polycentric language—i.e., a language with more than one standard form—or 'three languages for the price of one' (see p. 27). In spite of the shared linguistic origin of these varieties which are largely intercommunicable, their speakers have often followed different paths that put them at odds with each other. More often than not, religion, opposing military alliances, and cultural traditions politically outweighed linguistic similarities.

Already Max Weber, in his discussion of language conflicts, mentions the volatile situation on the Balkans, pointing out that a common language may be 'insufficient in sustaining a sense of national identity. [...] Aside from the examples of the Serbs and Croats, [...] there are qualitative degrees of the belief in common nationality' (Weber 1968: 395). Insufficient in sustaining a sense of national identity, on the one hand, and harnessed to this very end, on the other—for this apparently contradictory attitude to a common language Yugoslavia has many examples to offer.

Josip Broz Tito, successful leader of the anti-Axis resistance during World War II, briefly established the unified Socialist Federal Republic where linguistic convergence was promoted to make 'Serbo-Croatian' the dominant language of all Yugoslavs. The truce between the biggest language groups did not last long, however, and in the convulsions of the 1990s disintegration driven by rekindled nationalisms, the post-Yugoslav states Croatia, Serbia, Bosnia, and Montenegro reinvented 'Yugoslavia's main official language, Serbo-Croatian [...] anew as the four separate national languages of Bosnian, Croatian, Montenegrin and Serbian' (Kamusella 2010: 335). Slovenia in the north of the country bordering Austria was first to break away from the Federal Republic and was least involved in the violence of the Yugoslav wars of the 1990s, while the other former republics descended into turmoil. Where were the borders between them to be drawn? In addition to speaking different linguistic varieties, the population of former Yugoslavia is divided by ethnic, religious, and cultural fault lines, and there was much overlap between groups, which is why the break-up of Yugoslavia was so contentious and marked by horrific violence. A South Slavic nation united in one state by one language turned out to be an illusion.

In spite of the genetic closeness and intercommunicability of the South Slavic languages, other historically grown differences between the various groups could not be erased from collective memory—Orthodox Christians in the east and Roman Catholics in the west; Christian heirs to the Habsburg Empire in the north and Muslim heirs to the Ottoman Empire in the south, to mention but the most conspicuous legacies, the divisive power of which is still felt today. The Dayton Peace Agreement of November 1995 brought an end to the war, although ethnic cleansing continued and, in some parts, resurged, notably in Kosovo where thousands of Kosovar Albanians fell victim to Serbian forces. In contrast to the differences between the South Slavic varieties, the differences between Serbian and Albanian are profound, so that they are not intercommunicable. This is a part of the problem of the still unresolved situation in Kosovo.

Against this backdrop, the language conflicts that accompanied Yugoslavia's break-up and the language policy measures adopted to install new national languages seem contrived, but they were as much part of the hostilities as of the peace agreement. The Dayton Accords were written and signed in Serbian, Croatian and Bosnian, and from then on official documents in post-war Bosnia have been redacted in three versions.[14] The differences between them even trained editors have a hard time to sort out and the users may not always readily recognize each other as speakers of one or the other. Meanwhile, Croatia cultivated linguistic purism to eliminate all Serbian (dialect) influence from Croatian. In Serbia, where traditionally the Cyrillic alphabet is identified with Serbian but the Latin alphabet is also widely used, script choice became a major issue. And in Bosnia-Herzegovina Arabic and Turkish loanwords were worked on as a distinctive feature of the Bosnian language.

Controversies about the relationship between Yugoslav successor languages continued. However, ironically, the emphasized differences notwithstanding, none of the language groups has relinquished Štokavian, the high-prestige dialect shared by Croatian, Serbian, Montenegrin, and Bosnian, to elevate a local low-prestige variety to new national standard instead. Is Montenegrin then a Serbian dialect? The answer is in the eyes of the beholders and differs depending on whether they are disinterested linguists or politicians.

Looking back at the language policy dynamics on the post-World War II Balkans, it can be said that, on the surface, the linguistic unification of the country officially underwritten by the Yugoslav state failed, but at the same time the proclamation of new national languages has not eradicated basic commonalities and far-reaching mutual communicability. The legal inauguration of new national languages in the Yugoslavian successor states was largely symbolic, as language policy, especially status planning, so often is.

Pakistan

Even with the brutality of the Yugoslav War in mind, it is hard to think of a new state coming into existence engulfed by more terrifying violence than Pakistan. Indian intellectuals had campaigned for independence for decades, and when the British realized that they no longer had the resources to control the subcontinent, they withdrew hastily and without much preparation. When the curtain fell on Britain's biggest colony in 1947, what for centuries had been a hybrid Indo-Islamic civilization distinguished by vivid multilingualism and languages which infused Sanskrit-derived vernaculars with Persian, Arabic, and Turkish lexemes, was swamped by waves of unimaginable bloodshed that left between 1 and 2 million people dead and an estimated 15 million displaced. The reasons for the traumatic riots, massacres, expulsions, and resettlements triggered by the partition are the subject of a profuse literature, which is not here the place to examine.

Three contributing factors to the chaos in the wake of Britain's withdrawal were borders, ideologies, and personalities. For a long time, partition was not on the agenda of the leaders of the anti-colonial independence movement. The most prominent personalities, Mohandas Gandhi and Jawaharlal Nehru, representing the Hindu-dominated Congress Party, and Muhammad Ali Jinnah, leader of the Muslim League, envisioned one Indian state and did not plan for divisions along religious lines. Jinnah favoured a secular state, but partly driven by mutual dislike of Gandhi and Nehru who dominated negotiations with the British, he came to demand a Muslim homeland—with disastrous effects. Hindus and Muslims became increasingly polarized and mixed neighbourhoods where people used to live in harmony became dangerous to live in. It was only then that plans for two successor states began to be made. Cyril Radcliffe, a British judge, had only a few weeks for drawing the borders of the two new states, which he actually announced two days after India's independence on 15 August 1947.

The resulting separation of a Hindustan and a Pakistan was artificial and, as some said, untannable because Pakistan consisted of two provinces, West Pakistan and East Pakistan, divided by a thousand miles of Indian territory. But since the partition and the violence it instigated pitted religious communities against each other, a Pakistani nation seemed to be emerging, with Jinnah as its leader. As advocate of Muslim minority rights in British India, he was respected in Bengal in the east as much as in Punjab, Sindh, and other regions in the west. Actually, Jinnah was an unlikely head of an Islamic state. He was a British educated barrister secularist married to a non-Muslim woman and had little interest in Muslim clerics. Yet he supported Islam, which he saw as binding western and eastern population groups and the millions of refugees who fled India together. An international religion that had taken root in many parts of the world was not enough to sustain a state. Soon after the partition language thus became a political issue.

Jinnah adopted the European idea of unity of language and state, at least in the sense that a state must have a language for all. In the spring of 1948, he went to the eastern province and on 21 March addressed a large audience at Dhaka University where he warned against destroying the unity of Pakistan by undermining the language regime he had in mind. People were free, he argued, to use any language of their choice, but 'there can only be one state language if the component parts of this state are to march forward in unison and that language, in my opinion, can only be Urdu.' It was a long speech in which he repeated several times that there would be only one state language of Pakistan with all its component parts, including, of course, East Bengal, [...] 'because without one state language, no nation can remain tied up solidly together and function.'[15]

Jinnah's speech did not go down well with all of his listeners, but at the time few would have said that it marked the beginning of the end of the Pakistan he had founded. Ever since independence there had been a movement to promote Bangla (Bengali) in East Pakistan, which was greatly strengthened by Jinnah's harsh criticism as undermining the unity of Pakistan. Resistance in East Pakistan against Urdu as sole state language was understandable because with the exception of refugees from Urdu-speaking regions in India the population did not speak it. Bengali, a highly cultivated language with a long literary tradition in Buddhism, Hinduism, and Islam, was the native language of the overwhelming majority of East Pakistanis who, moreover, significantly outnumbered West Pakistanis, yet should accept Urdu as their national language which was much more at home in the West.

Jinnah's emphasis on the need of one and only one state language kindled opposition. By way of setting its LP goals, the East demanded federal status for Bengali alongside Urdu and English, protested the removal of the Bengali script from bank notes and stamps, and demanded that Bengali be used as language of instruction in all of East Pakistan's schools. Over the next 24 years, the language conflict would not die down. On 21 February, 1952 police opened fire on a pro-Bengali rally in Dhaka, killing five activists and injuring hundreds of others. Commemorating this tragedy, the United Nations General Assembly in 2002 designated this day as Mother Language Day.[16] Eventually, Jinnah's misguided language policy led to the break-up of Pakistan and, after another horrific armed conflict, led to the foundation of Bangladesh as an independent republic, where Bengali became the official and national language.

Needless to say, but a matter of interest, since no one in Dhaka understood Urdu, Jinnah delivered his 1948 speech to promote Urdu as Pakistan's only national language there in English, not his first language but one of which he had a perfect command. The world he had grown up in was thoroughly multilingual. His L1 was Gujarati, and Urdu he acquired later without ever reaching in any of these two a level of proficiency comparable to his English. Language to him was a matter of choice and Urdu should be chosen as Pakistan's sole national language because, as he argued, it embodied the best of Muslim culture, for the East as much as for the West. However, his own experience may have made him underestimate the emotional forces set free when language enters the realm of politics. In East Pakistan Urdu was and remained the language of domineering West Pakistan rather than the language of the country as a whole.

Urdu, a hybrid language that carries with it the interwoven heritage of Sanskrit, Persian, Arabic, and Turkish, was cherished by Jinnah as symbol of the culture on which a new state could be erected, geographically divided though it was. Today, it is Pakistan's national language, sharing official status with English. It didn't take long for Urdu to be reduced in the imagination of many to the language of Pakistan only, conveniently ignoring the Urdu speech community of some 50 million in India. Officially, Urdu is recognized as a language of India along with 21 others in the eighth schedule of the Indian Constitution.[17] The majority of Indian Urdu speakers are Muslims, although there are also Sikhs and Hindus, but the pigeonholing thinking of linguistic nationalism ignores them. That Urdu is intimately bound up with the history of India where it evolved over centuries is forgotten, as is the fact that Jawaharlal Nehru, the great Hindu hero of Indian independence, was an admirer and fluent speaker of it. The association of Urdu with Pakistan and Islam has in recent decades made it the target of discrimination and hostility by Hindu nationalists who would change place names in Urdu, protest the teaching of Urdu at school, and instruct their children to tell their classmates to take their Urdu mother tongue 'back' to Pakistan, where they and their parents have never lived. In January 2020, Urdu signboards of railway stations in the northern Indian state Uttarakhand were replaced with Sanskrit. Given that L1 speakers—to use a less emotionally charged term than mother-tongue speakers—of Sanskrit are a few hundred in the state, while more than 400,000 speak Urdu, this could only be seen as an act of anti-Muslim discrimination on the part of the right-wing ruling Bharatiya Janata Party, and, from the point of view of the uninvolved observer, as yet another example of politically motivated language attitudes that have nothing whatever to do with the substance of the language concerned, but everything with the ideas and ideologies imposed on it.

Summing up

Ever since language conflicts became a by-product of nationalism and the European nation state system, language policy has become increasingly important as a force in the broader field of policy development propelling structural reforms and in some cases state reconfigurations. We have in this chapter briefly reviewed five cases of language conflicts. Two of them could be resolved more or less successfully or, better, could be limited to simmering on a small flame. In Belgium and Canada, lengthy negotiations and the willingness to compromise helped to overcome the main language cleavages and the speech communities involved are living together more peacefully for the time being than only a few decades ago, but language policy issues have not been erased from the national agenda of either country and could disrupt everyday politics at any time. The poisonous dogma of linguistic nationalism—about which more in the next chapter—is hard to overcome even in affluent countries where multilingualism is both common and widely supported. Affluence can make it easier to deal with the costs multilingualism inevitably brings with it for education and administration, among others; but, as can be concluded from our third example, it is no safeguard against the emergence of new language-related discords. The main reason for increasing migration from Latin American countries to the United States in recent decades is the wealth gap between the two. Resented by many English-speaking whites, this demographic development has turned Spanish into a language policy challenge that can no longer be ignored.

In the remaining two cases, erstwhile Yugoslavia and Pakistan, language policy resulted in disaster bringing horrifying inter-group strife and the break-up of polities in its train. What makes both situations so hard to explain is that coexisting with speakers of different languages/varieties and sharing languages in a multilingual environment was historically a well-known pattern in both cases. It is shocking that dislike of others can degenerate to the point of barbarism, as it did in the Yugoslav war of the 1990s and the turmoil of the Partition of India, and that language plays a major part in this. In both cases, language was overlaid by religion as a group-defining feature, which undoubtedly aggravated the conflict. Language alone may be instrumentalized for nationalism, but then it cannot be imposed at will, as in the case of East Pakistan, or be insufficient for holding together a polity marked by other counter currents, as in the case of Yugoslavia where religious affiliation and historical heritage undermined national unity. Both language and religion can be put at the service of the nation, at times to terrible effect, because those who are trying to make history do not always know what they are doing. Jinnah's fervent advocating of Urdu as Pakistan's national language is an unsettling example. This is one of the reasons why the relationship between language(s) and nation is often hard to untangle.

Further reading

Anwary, Afroza. 2011. Frame alignment and the dynamics of the national language movement of East Pakistan. *Journal of Asian History* Vol. 45: 163–191.

Geerts, Guido. 2011. Language legislation in Belgium and the balance of power in Walloon-Flemish relationships. In Roeland van Hout and Uus Knops (eds.), *Language Attitudes in the Dutch Language Area*. Berlin, New York: De Gruyter Mouton, 2011, pp. 25–38.

Kamusella, Tomasz, Motoki Nomachi, and Catherine Gibson (eds.) 2015. *The Palgrave Handbook of Slavic Languages, Identities and Borders*. London: Palgrave.

Heller, Monica. 2003. *Crosswords: Language, Education, and Ethnicity in French Ontario*. Berlin, New York: Mouton de Gruyter.

Macías, R. F. 2014. Spanish as the second national language of the United States: fact, future, fiction, or hope? *Review of Research in Education* 38(1), 33–57. https://doi.org/10.3102/0091732X13506544

4

Normalization and standardization

Language as an artefact

> Indeed, it makes quite a big difference whom you tell about the end of the standard language. Those who react with annoyance and anger generally belong to older generations; many younger people do not mind that much. Or, when they understand what the standard language used to be, they often react positively. The old Renaissance fear of Babel is notably waning in our days. It's still there, for sure, but no longer with everyone. Thus, it probably won't be for long. And this, too, can be seen as part of the transition from one language culture to another (Van der Horst 2008: 304, translated FC).

Writing

Language works because each language is a rule-governed system and its speakers have internalized and follow the rules of the system. To say that they have internalized the rules means that they have learned them, by and large, without explicit instruction in early childhood by hearing others speak. Considering the fact that languages are highly complex systems, of which we become aware once as adults we learn additional languages with the help of textbooks or online courses, the effortless language acquisition of children without instruction is nothing short of miraculous. Just as they learn their first language(s) without being

Language Policy. Florian Coulmas, Oxford University Press. © Florian Coulmas (2025).
DOI: 10.1093/9780191976377.003.0004

taught, they gradually change them to be able to express whatever they want and need to communicate. There are other factors that drive change, such as, for example, wear and tear—if 'good' is no longer good enough, it's 'super', then 'mega', and so forth—however, on the whole language change happens incrementally without us noticing it and without being announced. Language is in constant flux, for speech disappears as soon as it is uttered.

All of this changes with grammar. As linguists use the term today, all languages, dialects and other variants function on the basis of their inherent grammar, but in an earlier understanding which is still common today among non-linguists, grammar is a written code that applies to written language. The etymology of the term is reminiscent of that. Greek *grammatikē (tekhnē)* means the '(art of) letters'. There is thus a close link between grammar and writing. Until very recently, when oral languages of very small speech communities became topical, a subject to which we will turn in Chapter 11, language policy dealt with grammar in this sense and with written language. To put it differently, language policy is to do with (at least partly) literate society, the promotion of literacy often being one of its objectives. Literacy is never taught in the abstract, but inevitably as the ability to read and write a particular language.

Providing an unwritten language with a writing system has been called 'reducing it to writing'. This is a misleading expression inasmuch as writing, rather than reduce, greatly expands the expressive potential of language. True, oral transmission of lengthy poems and other works are well-attested and quite impressive, however, there are countless things that can be done in writing but not in speech. Think of 'don't kill the messenger!' for instance, an expression that speaks of oral communication where the separation of message from messenger is less common, even harder to conceive, than in a society where it would never occur to you to blame the postman for a letter with unpleasant contents. Think of the 'literal' meaning of a word which, it can be argued, only exists where it can be fixed. Where can it be fixed? In dictionaries, of course. And think of calendars, scriptures, legal codes, novels, PhD theses, passports, etc., all of which exist in writing only. The invention of writing and its introduction into a community is a most consequential occurrence that changes its way of life and its language. Carved in stone, put down on parchment or paper with a brush or pencil, printed and downloadable from the internet, it has a range of qualities that distinguishes it from the fleeting spoken word.

On the other hand, saying that a language is 'being reduced to writing' captures an important consequence of all this, that is, the stability and permanence of writing as opposed to the fluidity of speech. Writing reduces variation. Writing makes of languages countable objects with which among many other things language policy can take issue. The fact that human beings learn their first language(s) without instruction gives rise to the question what kind of objects languages are. Since every child can acquire any language, languages have been associated with natural species. At the same time, they change for reasons that resemble societal changes more than natural evolution triggered by selection pressure. So, are languages things of their own kind, neither natural nor societal? This question continues to occupy scholarship. However, in contradistinction to language, there is no vagueness or uncertainty about writing being an artefact. Writing systems do not come into existence as the result of natural forces of development, but every single one has been crafted by imaginative people, and they are cultivated further through human intervention.

Writing makes languages manageable, both with regard to how speakers use them and, most importantly, what they consist of. In one way or another writing relates to language. How exactly a particular writing system W^x is related to a particular language L^x is a historical and structural matter that need not concern us here; but the relationship itself makes it necessary to be able to say what is L^x, or to reduce the many forms of oral L^x to one, or to draw lines in the continuum of varieties of which it consists stipulating that L^x extends from a to b and that everything outside this extent is not L^x. Counting languages, as every linguist knows, is a task that, because one variety fades into the other and dialect continua may include mutually non-intelligible varieties, is all but impossible to carry out without making some arbitrary decisions. Some of the examples discussed in the previous chapter have moreover shown that the judgements and desires of speakers can be decisive factors determining where L^x ends and where L^y begins. But drawing the lines is usually impossible without drawing lines, that is, without writing. To put things into perspective, it may be useful to note that the majority of all languages are never used in writing, even if they have been given a writing system by a linguist or missionary.

Norms and standardization

In order to live together peacefully, people need norms that regulate their behaviour. There are implicit norms or conventions that most people follow out of habit or cultivated tradition; and there are explicit norms that take on the form of codified law. Similarly, in language and communication traditional conventions of usage and overtly declared norms coexist. Likening standard grammars and legal codes is more than a fleeting allegory. Both distinguish right from wrong in ways that philosophers of law and language have tried in vain to trace back unequivocally to nature (natural law) or a higher spiritual power (divine law), but which are nonetheless designed to regulate human behaviour.

Writing is the indispensable tool for setting linguistic norms, and grammars, dictionaries, and spelling books are the principal means of embodying them. Looking at the years when the first grammars of some languages were written and published (Table 2), the historicity of these accomplishments becomes apparent. We are looking at the Renaissance as it evolved and at the age of European expansion, most symbolically represented by the publication in 1492 of Antonio Nebrija's grammar of Castilian Spanish. Nebrija saw in his work a political act for which he eventually, after some persuasion, received his queen's backing. The point at issue was to elevate the status of Castilian on a par with Latin, the language not just of learning but of everything that was important. Like all languages in Europe, Castilian coexisted with Latin in a situation of functional domain division which would much later be called 'diglossia', a term first introduced by William Marçais (1930) and popularized by Charles Ferguson (1959).

Table 2 First grammars of select languages

The first grammar of	Year of appearance	Author and title
Spanish	1492	Antonio de Nebrija, *Gramática de la lengua castellana*
Italian	1516	Giovani Francesco Fortunio, *Regole grammaticali della volgar lingua*
German	1534	Valentin Ickelsamer, *Teutsche Grammatica*
French	1550	Louis Maigret, *Tretté de la Grammaire française*
Dutch	1568	Johan Radermacher, *Voorreden vanden noodich ende nutticheit der Nederduytscher taalkunste*
English	1586	William Bullokar, *Pamphlet for Grammar*
Indonesian	1948	Sutan Takdir Alisjahbana, *Tatabahasa Baru Bahasa Indonesia*

Diglossic situations are characterized by a division of labour between a **h**igh-prestige variety, H, used for formal affairs, notably government, church, and learning, and vernacular or **l**ow-prestige varieties, L, used for commerce and everyday conversation. It was fundamentally also a division between written and spoken language, and since literacy was socially stratified and the H domains were largely reserved for socially segregated groups, the diglossia of the time had a strong class aspect.

The remarkable case of Bahasa Indonesia

In retrospect, overcoming diglossia can be seen as an integral part of European nation building and modernization, which among other developments included stronger social integration and elevating the language of the common people by giving it a written form. It was a gradual transition from a class- and function-specific use of a dominant written language and an indeterminate number of oral varieties to an all-purpose national language for everyone. Looking now at the last row of Table 2, the year of the first grammar of Bahasa Indonesia, the national language of Indonesia today, stands in stark contrast to that of the other grammars listed there. Why the hiatus of more than four centuries? This is a rhetorical question because the answer is obvious. Nation building in what used to be the Netherlands East Indies only took off once Portuguese, Dutch, and, in the final little episode, Japanese colonizers had left the archipelago and a common written language uniting its inhabitants with their 800-odd tongues was deemed necessary. Bahasa Indonesia is a standardized variant of Malay which had for centuries served them as a lingua franca and was therefore not considered an imposed foreign language. Having grown up in the Netherlands East Indies, writer Sutan Takdir Alisjahbana maintained overall positive views of European modernism and perceived the need for independent Indonesia to articulate itself in a national language.

This, Alisjahbana and like-minded intellectuals understood, required more than a symbolic declaration. A lingua franca with loose ends, vague boundaries, and no standards of right and wrong is not suitable for higher education, a systematic collection of statutes, legal procedures, and political negotiations. In the past, other highly elaborate varieties of Malay had been used by court circles of the sultanates in Sumatra and on the Malay peninsula, but they were obsolete and far removed from the 'market-Malay' people spoke. The upgrading and standardization of Bahasa Indonesia was, therefore, a project of great political importance. Alisjahbana did not accomplish it by himself, however, his grammar and his many publications contributed a great deal and are held in high esteem in Indonesia to this day.[1] While structuralist linguistics which distanced itself from the normative ideas of traditional philology flourished in Europe, he emphasized the importance of prescriptive grammar and lexicography which he felt were being neglected by academic linguists. Norms must be stable, well-founded, and avoid uninformed stipulations. Whoever is charged with this task of norm-setting must be well-versed in the language at issue and able to select the most suitable rules and forms among the various alternatives that are available. Alisjahbana had been working on this since the 1920s and helped to make Bahasa Indonesia a key symbol of the independence movement. He became the first secretary of the Indonesian Language Commission[2] established under Japanese rule in 1942 and continued to work on the development of Bahasa Indonesia after the Japanese had left and independence from the Netherlands had been achieved.

One of the challenges of turning Bahasa Indonesia into a functional national language was the almost complete lack of a technical vocabulary for science and administration. New terms had to be coined or borrowed by the thousands, preferably without provoking feelings of alienation and the idea that the language was being corrupted. The history of the Indonesian archipelago has seen many invaders and merchants in tangible and spiritual goods which left traces in the Malay language. Hinduism and Buddhism came from the Indian subcontinent with Sanskrit as an important sacred language. In the course of the Islamic expansion Arabic became a major influence, including the writing of Malay in Arabic letters for some time. Centuries of Portuguese, Dutch, and British colonization followed, while Chinese immigrants brought Hokkien, Cantonese, Hakka, and other Chinese vernaculars to Java and Sumatra since the late eighteenth century. There was, moreover, a wealth of Indigenous languages, among them some highly cultivated ones with a long literary tradition, notably Javanese spoken by 30–45 per cent of Indonesians. There are thus many sources to draw from for the lexical enrichment of Bahasa Indonesia. New terms were needed for various fields of specialized knowledge, which required the expertise of scholars in these fields who knew what the terms mean, what they should mean, and how best the intended meaning could be expressed. In addition to that, sensitivities about these various sources must be taken into account: in order to avoid inter-community strife, Bahasa Indonesia must not be Javanized too strongly. New loanwords should/should not make use of internationalisms, because they will bring the language up to date, or because they will undermine its authenticity. Roman letters should be used and the spelling should be modelled on Dutch rather than English because it is so much more regular and hence easier to learn. Coining new words is to be preferred to borrowing, or vice versa, depending on one's commitment to preserve purity or easy connection, etc. The Language Commission dealt with these issues in regular meetings where the standardization and codification of the grammar was likewise systematically deliberated over many years.

When, upon the proclamation of independence in 1945, Bahasa Indonesia was declared Indonesia's national language, the work was far from finished, but well on its way to spread the language throughout society as the principal means to accommodate the linguistic, ethnic, and religious diversity of the population in a unified state. To this, the Japanese occupiers may have contributed unwittingly. In January 1942, they drove the Dutch out of the East Indies and then stayed there for just a bit more than three years. They outlawed the Dutch language and, since they could not expect the 'liberated'[3] population to learn Japanese overnight, embraced Bahasa Indonesia, which some, including Alisjahbana, saw as the decisive impetus for its dispersion throughout the archipelago—one couldn't say 'throughout the nation', for this was a two-way process of creating the nation in tandem with the national language.

Bahasa Indonesia was made a subject of compulsory education which in addition to promoting it in the media and other publications became the main engine of its spread. The school, teaching it as a subject and using it increasingly as medium of instruction, was the crucial institution of Indonesia's language diffusion policy. The population proficient in the language thus grew from year to year. To quote a reliable figure for the proportion with a good command of the language is difficult—estimates range up to 90 per cent—but there is no doubt about the status of Bahasa Indonesia today. It is the main language of education, government, business, and the media.

In view of the fact that Indonesia is in the post-colonial world quite exceptional in using one of its own languages rather than a remnant of colonial times for higher education and in other elite domains, turning Bahasa Indonesia into the country's uncontested national language was a major achievement. Since in one and the same socio-political setting languages never coexist on an equal footing, this would have been impossible without a goal-oriented and clearly designed language policy. For the same reason, that they do not coexist on an equal footing, elevating the status of one language cannot but have consequences for others. Status planning for Bahasa Indonesia profoundly changed the sociolinguistic configuration of this multilingual country. For one thing, compared to English, French, Spanish, and Portuguese in post-colonial countries, Dutch had no weighty future in independent Indonesia. The Dutch East India Company and then the colonial government had never done much to promote it in the population and then it was suddenly decommissioned by decree. Even though many public servants spoke Dutch and official documents were in Dutch, it did not stand in the way of Bahasa Indonesia to assume the function of official language. With it a vernacular that used to be one among others, though more widely used as a link language, became the object of deliberate moulding and was now endowed with the prestige of officialdom bringing about new kinds of relations between the languages of the archipelago by occupying the high position. Will this lead to the demise of many of these minor languages? Alisjahbana preferred to say that Bahasa Indonesia 'absorbed' many of the local languages rather than drove them out of use. Whatever you call it, assigning a language a privileged status—that of national language to Bahasa Indonesia—is likely to, and actually has in many cases, put minor languages under pressure (Hamied and Musthafa 2019 for more details).

In any event, the case of Bahasa Indonesia illustrates well that the implementation of language policy depends on many factors, including imponderables—such as Japan's brief intervention in the last phase of Indonesia's independence movement—and that it has various consequences, including unforeseen ones—such as the decline of minority languages. Suffice it here to mention the following five prerequisites that must supplement the language policy cycle model (p. 8):

- a clearly defined policy objective, such as the standardization of a language,
- a language that can satisfy this objective,
- determined and competent language activists,
- official backing in the form of a language regulating institution,
- a population that is ready to accept profound change in their language behaviour.

The Indonesian intellectuals who cultivated Bahasa Indonesia and established it as their national language knew what they were aiming at. They were as familiar with the linguistic multitude of their homeland as they were with the standard languages of powerful countries, and they knew that language was of great importance to the political process; for a national language was a crucial instrument of nation building (Montolalu and Suryadinata 2015). In Indonesia, the institutionalization of nation and national language happened in fast motion, so to speak, in a world where nation states were normal and viewed by many as a desirable or inevitable form of political organization, of which a national standard language was a vital part. In other parts of the world this was a long-drawn-out process.

Recording and regulating language

Like the nation, the national language is a construct. Its realization depends on recording and regulating a variety that was designated and at the same time created for this purpose by means of grammar books and dictionaries, an undertaking that is often but not always mandated by an explicit language policy. By recording and thereby setting rules and compiling words these works make languages manageable, as pointed out above, which means that the language in question can be taught and learned systematically and thus dispersed beyond the original population of its speakers. In Europe, this happened simultaneously and in connection with the gradual advance of literacy following the transition from woodblock to moveable type printing. Political scientist Benedict Anderson (1991) pointed out that this was a socio-political as much as an economic process and introduced the notion of 'print capitalism' to further the analytic understanding of it. Once the potential of the technology of moveable type was recognized in Europe, printers became a driving force in language standardization. As of the sixteenth century, the printing press both created and made it possible to address a market that transcended elitist literacies in Latin and other script languages of the upper classes. At the same time, choosing one language variety for printing was less laborious and hence more profitable than reproducing the diversity of vernaculars in print. The new industry could only benefit from a market that grew with an increasing population able to read texts of this variety, and by selling its products did much to afford that variety the status of standard. Economic incentives were thus among the factors that can explain the emergence of standard languages. Political considerations came into play by and by as literacy levels increased, dynastic absolutist regimes were gradually or, as in France, suddenly complemented or replaced by more popular political participation, and nationalism appeared on the intellectual horizon. Since it had been the unquestioned practice for centuries that the language of the court was not the same as that of the common people, it took time for language policies to be formed that focussed on spreading a vernacular as language of state in order to facilitate communication between ruler and ruled as well as laterally within the general population. Academies tasked with studying and stabilizing the dominant language, notably the Accademia della Crusca in Florence (1582), the Académie française in Paris (1635) and the Real Academia Española in Madrid (1713), gradually assumed more responsibilities for supervising and regulating the language. The decisive push for establishing and administrating a national standard language came with industrialization and general education.

The linguistic homogenization in the name of the national language progressed, first in Europe and then in other parts of the world, but the political trajectories differed. When and how compulsory education was implemented; if and when language regulators were instituted and what tasks they were assigned; to what extent such regulators became governmental bodies; how strong their influence was on the standardization of the language under their supervision—these and other specifics varied from country to country. There has never been a formal regulator of the English language, for example; yet, the linguistic homogenization of the country was on the political agenda, as attested by the British Parliament's decision in 1870 to remove Welsh from schools as a medium of instruction, a move that was much in line with the marginalization of minority languages in other European countries at the time.

To what extent the regulation of the language should be a state responsibility also differed across countries. For instance, if one compares

France and England, those inclined to do so can detect here the difference between a statist and a market economy approach almost clichéd. In France, Cardinal Richelieu (1585–1642), head of government and founder of the Académie française, defined one of its tasks as 'providing the language with exact rules, rendering it pure, eloquent and capable of dealing with the arts and sciences'.[4] Somewhat later in England, Samuel Johnson, considered the most influential lexicographer of his age and beyond until the beginning of the publication of the Oxford English Dictionary in 1884, was hired in 1746 by a group of London booksellers to write a comprehensive dictionary for which he would be paid the extraordinary sum of 1,500 guineas (purchasing power equivalent of about £260,000 in 2022). Fame or gain is a question that informs language policy in various ways, that will be discussed in more detail in Chapter 9.

The comparison of the language regimes in France and England draws attention to another parallel, namely to the legal systems of these countries, i.e., civil law and common law. In civil law systems such as France abstract principles and codified statues dominate court proceedings. Case law (also common law) systems, on the other hand, such as Britain tend to rely more on applying precedential legal opinions to current cases. The divisions between these two systems are not always clear cut, but they do reflect somewhat different legal attitudes and practices that can be compared to more rule-conscious and more usage-oriented language attitudes. In his 'Plan of a Dictionary of the English Language' Samuel Johnson actually made the similarity of his approach to common law explicit:

> Since the rules of stile, like those of law, arise from precedents often repeated, [I shall] collect the testimonies of both sides, and endeavour to discover and promulgate the decrees of custom, who has so long possessed whether by right or by usurpation, the sovereignty of words.

The contrast with Richelieu's view that the French language needed to be regulated in accordance with rational principles is quite apparent. In keeping with this directive, the 1660 Port-Royal Grammar by Antoine Arnauld and Claude Lancelot, which would be used as a textbook throughout France until the nineteenth century was called in its full title: *Grammaire générale et raisonnée contenant les fondemens de l'art de parler, expliqués d'une manière claire et naturelle* ('General and Rational Grammar, containing the fundamentals of the art of speaking, explained in a clear and natural manner'), where *raisonnée* referred to abstract principles of logical reasoning rather than precedents of usage. Language, that was the underlying idea, can be governed by logical principles and its speakers, too, can be made to follow them: language as the domain of reason.

Richelieu's mission statement seems to imply that the French language of his time did not have exact rules and was not pure, eloquent, and capable of dealing with the arts and sciences. Writing grammars and dictionaries, in this view, meant working for perfection, which raises the questions: perfection of what and for what? Jean-Baptiste Colbert, one-time prime minister and closely associated with the Académie française, knew the answer, which can be found in the preface of the first edition of the academy's dictionary. He wanted to see the dictionary completed, 'being persuaded, as the wisest politicians have been, that what serves to form eloquence contributes much to the glory of a Nation'. He recognized, though, that this was an incremental process, the perfection of the language progressing from one edition of the dictionary to the next.[5]

The parallelism of language and law has been observed by other lexicographers as well, although not necessarily affirmed, as in France, nor was perfecting their language or contributing to the glory of the nation their purpose. For instance, Wilhelm and Jacob Grimm set themselves the task of compiling a comprehensive dictionary of the German language, however, they stressed documentation above regimentation of the language. As Wilhelm put it, 'we do not want to produce a code of laws, but rather represent the language as it has represented itself over the course of three centuries', and thus present a 'natural history of the individual words, as it were'.[6] In the Grimms' understanding, language was more akin to natural phenomena obeying their own intrinsic laws rather than being susceptible to regulation by positive law. Notwithstanding this very different conceptualization of language, their dictionary reinforced the process of standardizing the German language because the Grimms concentrated on the umbrella language that had evolved over the past several centuries for written texts that all speakers of German should be able to understand and, therefore, avoided dialect forms.

French, English, and German had a written tradition when their first grammars and comprehensive dictionaries were planned and created and shared much of their culture. Regularization associated with print culture as expressed in official publications, schoolbooks, and newspapers led in all three cases to the emergence of a supra-local standard language free of dialectal features. This standard language has a written and a spoken form, but while in oral communication many speakers still use speech forms that reveal their regional background, the written language is unified. Norms of pronunciation have also been set, e.g., Received Pronunciation, especially for the theatre, but these norms usually refer to a written standard. In spite of these commonalities, coincidence of social history led the emergence of standard French, English, and German along different trajectories and resulted in three different models. Simply put, French is the most rigidly normative standard language based on the educated spoken and written registers of the Parisian variety; standard British English, anchored in London and southeast England, is more usage-oriented, while standard German never had the backing of the power and prestige of a metropolitan centre, but gradually evolved quasi 'naturally' by reducing dialectal features in writing. French, English, and German developed standard varieties that defined the position of these languages in the world, but would not eliminate their internal diversity. National varieties—Belgian, Swiss, Italian, Canadian French, Irish, North American, Australian, New Zealand, Indian English, Swiss, Austrian, Italian German—did not lose their distinctiveness. From a language policy point of view such diversity in unity contributes to the relative strength of these languages.

While these three models differ in many ways from each other, they all accompanied, and are important aspects of, the modernization of Europe, which, as the example of Indonesia has illustrated, had many implications for language policies not just in Europe, but throughout the world. These various policies are informed and justified by language ideologies relating to state, nation, social cohesion, citizenship, among others, and therefore warrant closer inspection. The next chapter gives an overview of language ideologies, how they came into existence and have an influence on politics, before we will then turn to the agencies that were created in order to study, regulate, promote, or prohibit languages in the spirit of these ideologies.

Further reading

Alisjahbana, S. Takdir. 1984. The concept of language standardization and its application to the Indonesian language. In Florian Coulmas (ed.) *Linguistic Minorities and Literacy: Language Policy Issues in Developing Countries*. Berlin, Boston: De Gruyter Mouton: 77–98. https://doi.org/10.1515/9783110865301.77

Anderson, Benedict. 1991. *Imagined Communities: Reflections on the Origin and Spread of Nationalism*. Revised edition. London: Verso.

Coulmas, Florian. 2016. *Guardians of Language. Twenty Voices Through History*. Oxford: Oxford University Press.

5

Language ideologies

> ROME, 31 March (Reuters)—Prime Minister Giorgia Meloni's party has proposed imposing fines of up to 100,000 euros ($108,750) on public and private entities which use foreign terms, most notably English, instead of Italian in official communications. 31 March 2023[1]
>
> Fabio Rampelli, member of the right-wing nationalist party *Fratelli d'Italia*, in 2022 proposed a law that would prohibit the use of any other language than Italian in official documents. In an interview with *Corriere della Sera* he explained that globalization posed a threat to the Italian language and that 'protecting our history, from Latin to Dante, means defending a cornerstone of our cultural identity'. *Corriere della Sera*, 2 April 2023[2]

Since language is indispensable for the formation of society and a part of the social experience, a means for interaction as well as for self-expression, people have beliefs and theories about language, what it is, what it does, how it is learned, etc. Taken together these beliefs and theories constitute language ideologies which like other belief systems characterize societies. An ideology in this sense is a body of shared knowledge, neither good nor bad, rather than a prejudiced doctrine. Language ideologies can be biased and grounded in false consciousness; however, I am using the term descriptively, assuming that there is no society that has no language ideology. Language ideologies are sometimes made explicit, but they typically include suppositions that

Language Policy. Florian Coulmas, Oxford University Press. © Florian Coulmas (2025).
DOI: 10.1093/9780191976377.003.0005

are taken for granted and never discussed, having been internalized in earliest childhood. It is therefore difficult to talk about language in an ideology-neutral manner, since the entire terminology is imbued with a certain perspective. This does not usually impede understanding, but sometimes the ideological character of an expression comes to the fore, as some examples may illustrate.

Mother tongue is an inconspicuous term that we use without thinking twice. It suggests something that everybody has: intimacy, nature, confidence. It is typically used in singular form; for like we have only one mother we have only one mother tongue—and this is where the ideological nature of the term becomes noticeable. That people have only one mother tongue is an idea and an ideal that does not reflect everybody's reality. Yet, many national censuses used to include a question about the respondents' mother tongue which required a single answer. Only in the last few decades have national surveys, which collect information about citizens, been modified in some countries to allow multiple answers to such a question and thereby paint a more realistic picture of a society's linguistic configuration. For instance, explanatory notes in the Canadian Census of Population 2021 show how outdated the concept of a single mother tongue is, revealing its ideological and political character:

> Mother tongue refers to the first language learned at home in childhood and still understood by the person at the time the data was collected. If the person no longer understands the first language learned, the mother tongue is the second language learned. For a person who learned more than one language at the same time in early childhood, the mother tongue is the language this person spoke most often at home before starting school. The person has more than one mother tongue only if they learned these languages at the same time, and still understands them.[3]

Or consider the case of Singapore where 'greater emphasis was placed on the prescription of mother-tongues, in the belief that "a race = a culture = a language"'. The meanings of the term are thus 'restricted within the parameters of functional polarization'.[4]

In these views, 'mother tongue' needs to be defined, for it can be one or many; it can be the first or second language learned in childhood, but not at school; it can be forgotten; it can be chosen; and it can be assigned to a 'race'. These are very different mother tongues from the unchanging once-and-for-all mother tongue acquired and spoken in an immobile world. Ideological terms are often adapted for specific purposes and therefore even more time-bound in their meaning than any words. Alternative terms such as 'L1', 'first language', 'dominant language', and 'home language', which are less emotionally charged and point to a multilingual reality, are used in academic discourse to circumvent such bias.

Sacred language is a term whose ideological nature is obvious—at least to those who have not been raised in a world where the veneration of a particular language as a manifestation of the sacred is part of normal life. That religious functions such as prayer, praise, and homily are to be performed in a language or variety removed from everyday conversation is assumed in many communities. The importance of language for human life is underlined in religious doctrines and cosmologies, where by being perceived as, or declared, sacred, language is assigned a world-ordering function. In the Biblical creation myth god turned chaos into order by calling light 'day' and dark 'night'. In Sanskrit, Vāc is the goddess of speech and as such a symbol of language as the foundation of the universe. In book religions not only the content but also the language in which the spiritual messages are formulated became revered as an object to be protected from improper use and alteration. Separated from popular use, these languages in the course of time developed a holy aura, like Classical Hebrew, Pāli—the holy language of Theravada Buddhism—Sanskrit, and Quranic or Classical Arabic. In these and some other cases the exclusive use of a language in a specific domain gave it a special character within the social repertoire. No language (variety) is inherently sacred, but an ideology can make it so.

National language. The same can be said about national languages which, however, since national communities and national states are much younger than religious communities are of a more recent conceptual origin than sacred languages. In a sense, they have replaced sacred languages as society has modernized and secularized where they became an object of veneration. Although sometimes portrayed as natural endowments of the nation, national languages are the result of politically motivated status planning, that is, of being singled out for this function and then cultivated through corpus planning to fulfil it. What exactly a national language is and how it interacts with other languages spoken in the nation state in question differs from country to country, once again underscoring the ideological character of the notion.

Ethnic language. A vernacular qualifies as an ethnic language if designated as such by speakers of dominant languages. Would French, English, or Dutch ever be ethnic languages? That is like asking whether pâté de foie gras or apple pie ought to be categorized as ethnic food. Even in environments where French, English, Dutch, or any other European national language is spoken by a small minority only, this is highly unlikely. 'Ethnic' means small, marginal, not mainstream, not being dominant anywhere, and perhaps exotic, from the point of view of those who do not belong to the communities so qualified but are in a position to determine terminology. Where multi-ethnic societies are discussed, the majority population is usually not included among the constituent groups. Accordingly, ethnic languages can by definition never be majority languages. That recognizing a variety as an ethnic language can nonetheless be a contentious issue is, on one hand, due to the notorious difficulty of counting languages and, on the other, to the fact that this difficulty is not usually resolved without the help of a language ideology.

Language death. Linguistic vitality, language life, and revitalization are concepts commonly used in sociolinguistics. They all relate to the same metaphor and the conceptualization of languages as living organisms, as does language death. Whatever can die must first live. The concept of language death overlooks or downplays the cultural, that is, artificial, character of languages as products of human work. Language activists choose such a conceptualization deliberately in order to draw attention to and thus perhaps help to resist what they perceive as a fatal trend in the age of globalization and neoliberalism where small-scale enterprises—read: languages—have a hard time surviving (see Chapter 10). Regardless of whether or not one views this choice of terminology favourably, its ideological motivation is obvious.

Many other terms could be adduced here in order to illustrate ideologically loaded discourses in the field of tension between linguistics and politics. The above five should suffice to show that this is not a fringe phenomenon or an aberration, but an expression of the great social and political importance of language, which makes it difficult and undesirable for many to discuss it in neutral terms. Against this backdrop let us now examine a couple of influential language ideologies in more detail in terms of how they underpin and are reflected in language policies.

Linguistic nationalism

Associating a nation with a language or defining the former with the latter is a conspicuous feature of modernity, at least of European modernization that from the seventeenth to the nineteenth century resulted in the establishment of national states. The linguistic nationalism that accompanied or grew out of this development appears in many varieties and can be observed in many places. The paradigm case is Germany.

The German language, as the philosopher Johann Gottlieb Fichte in his famous 1807 Addresses to the German Nation conceptualized it, appears as the 'mother tongue' that gives birth to the 'fatherland'—for lack of anything else, one might surmise. For at the time, major European powers such as France, Britain, Spain, Russia, and the Netherlands were constituted as more or less well-defined nation states, while German-speaking or, at least largely German-speaking territories were divided in many kingdoms, principalities, and feudal domains that were loosely united in the multi-ethnic and multilingual Holy Roman Empire. In the early nineteenth century, this political structure fell apart, as internal differences were compounded under the external influence of revolutionary and then Napoleonic France. Fichte delivered his addresses in the Prussian capital of Berlin, which Napoleon's troops had captured in 1806. Rather than a plea to a nation that existed, it was an appeal to become one, based on a common language, even if for many linguistic commonality did not necessarily mean mutual intelligibility. Both nation and national language were more of a political projection than a description of reality. This characterizes political statements more generally, especially when they deal with the cultivation and normalization of language. Fichte did not pay much attention to the considerable regional linguistic differences that persisted across German-speaking areas, but highlighted the potential of a common language for a common cause.

Language was a vehicle. How important an element of nation building Fichte thought it was emerges when he discusses the integration of others (a topic, we may note in passing, that still regularly surfaces on language ideology agendas today):

> It does not matter if ever so many individuals of other race and other language are incorporated with the people speaking this language; provided [...] they remain without influence on the language [i.e., German, FC], until the time comes when they themselves have entered into the sphere of observation of the original people. Hence, they do not form the language; it is the language which forms them (Fichte 1922: 62).

In present-day parlance: outsiders/immigrants welcome, as long as they assimilate and do not claim the right to influence further social and linguistic developments. Just learn our language well enough for it to shape you!

The deterministic view that attributes to the individual language, rather than to human language as such, a mind-shaping power would become very influential, first at the hands of Fichte's contemporary philosopher Wilhelm von Humboldt, who greatly admired his addresses, and later in the twentieth century by American linguists Edward Sapir and Benjamin Lee Whorf, patron saints of the so-called Sapir-Whorf hypothesis which similarly poses that the structure of one's language influences one's world view, a tenet that still has many adherents nowadays, as we will see in Chapter 11.

Fichte's new education aimed at creating a national consciousness built on language and cultivating the moral will to help others based on the pleasure in knowledge for everyone. This was an education which would bring about more social equity and go beyond the education 'which in the past, as a rule, only the higher classes received' (Fichte 1922: 47). Again, Fichte assigned not language in general, but the German language an all-important role in realizing this kind of education: 'The language of this people is necessarily just what it is, and in reality this people does not express its knowledge, but its knowledge expresses itself out of the mouth of the people' (Fichte 1922: 56). Jacob Grimm, another influential intellectual of the time, recognized the social aspect of developing German as national language, which he considered an antidote to the reactionary attitudes of the aristocracy that had always used choice of language to keep a distance from their subjects.

Fichte's addresses were hugely influential, in Germany and beyond. Elevating the common language from necessary tool to national symbol and thereby fostering a national consciousness and promoting equality was an idea that fell on fertile ground in other parts of Europe as well. The darker side of this ideology emerged later when the national language was harnessed right before the chariot, as for instance in the title of a book by Eduard Engel, published more than a century after Fichte's addresses, which is also indicative of the time it takes for a language ideology to take hold and its durability: *Sprich Deutsch! Zum Hilfsdienst am Vaterland. Im vierten Jahr des Weltkrieges ums deutsche Dasein* ('Speak German! In support of the fatherland. In the fourth year of the World War for German existence').

First equality and then unity and segregation from others. A similar dynamic was unfolding in the second half of the nineteenth century in Italy, another European country that had been divided among several rulers for centuries where in the wake of the Risorgimento movement and the unification of the Italian state in the 1860s language became the defining criterion of uniting or rather forming the nation state. 'Irredentism' (from *terre irredente* 'unredeemed lands'), a term introduced by Giuseppe Mazzini, a writer and activist for the unification of Italy, was for some time the battle cry. What exactly it comprised varied somewhat with the occasion of its application, because while there were majority Italian-speaking territories on the Dalmatian coast, Italian was a minority language in parts of Alto-Adige (South Tyrol). According to irredentists both were to be 'liberated' and thus integrated in a unified Italian-speaking Italian state. Alto-Adige did become part of

Italy, although the integration was marked by decades of sometimes violent language conflicts between German speakers and Italian speakers. In Istria and Dalmatia, on the other hand, irredentist claims were met by a strong pan-Slavic national movement, and the contested territories became part of Croatia and then Yugoslavia (and then Croatia—see Chapter 3). What can be learned from the story of irredentism is that in the tangle of nationalistic demands and geopolitical strategies numerical majorities do not necessarily play a decisive role. Nowadays Italian nationalists, therefore, still bemoan the 'loss' of the Croatian seaport of Rijeka, or Fiume, as for instance the neo-fascist movement CasaPound prefers to call it. South Tyrol (Figure 3), on the other hand, has been pacified and now counts as a success story of institutionalized bilingualism in a nation state where the hard edges of linguistic nationalism could be smoothed out in lengthy negotiations for the benefit of all.

Linguistic nationalism and irredentism were ideologies that flourished in the nineteenth century, but when we look at the post-colonial world they seem hardly outdated. In Malaysia, for instance, 'belief in a national language as an effective instrument for integrating a culturally plural society and as synonymous with nation-building was enshrined in the Razak Report and has remained an integral part of official Malaysian thinking' (Watson 1983: 138f.). Similarly, about East African countries Madumulla, Bertocini, and Blommaert (1999: 309) observe: 'In almost every case, language was brought to stand in relation to issues of national unity, nation-building and identity politics.'

Linguistic separatism

The above examples illustrate that linguistic nationalism is an ideology widely employed for nation building. In a variant form, it can also be applied for language building. In this case, the reasoning, 'We speak a common language and therefore are a nation', is reversed to 'We are a separate group/nation and therefore speak a language (and not a substandard vernacular or dialect).' Noah Webster comes to mind, who published an American Dictionary of the English Language, because he was convinced that a self-respecting nation needed a national language.

Figure 3 Officially displayed bilingualism in Brixen/Bressanone, South Tyrol, Italy
Photograph: Florian Coulmas

Other examples include Norwegian as an offshoot from Danish and Luxembourgish, for which independence from German was claimed only in the twentieth century when in the 1930s many Luxembourgers wanted to distance themselves from anything German and turned their Moselle

Franconian dialect into the ausbau language Luxembourgish. This was a purely political decision, and since most Luxembourgers speak also German and many French, too, the symbolic aspects weigh heavier than the practical ones. Similarly, the Spanish Civil War (1936–1939) boosted the linguistic separatism of Catalan. Repressed under the Franco regime, the movement continued until, in train with Spain's transition to democracy in the late 1970s, Catalan was institutionalized as official language of the autonomous community of Catalonia. Although the lexical overlap with Castilian Spanish exceeds 85 per cent, a majority of Catalans are content to see Catalan occupy a secure place as a language in its own right alongside Spanish in education, bureaucracy, and everyday life. In this respect, the Catalan language policy has been successful, although the quest for status upgrading continues. Pressured by Catalan separatists, Prime Minister Pedro Sánchez in 2023 proposed to get Catalan, as well as Basque and Galician, recognized as official languages of the EU (Moens and Hernádez-Morales 2023). With some 8 million speakers, Catalan is bigger than at least eight officially recognized EU languages[5], a fact that has been repeatedly cited to support the claim for its recognition. However, Sánchez's request met with immediate resistance in Brussels, not just because of the cost, but also because such a decision would open the gates for lobbying for many other languages to be recognized. Catalan is associated with a long history of oppression which may be one reason why Catalan language activists vie for its recognition at the EU level. In Spain its status is no longer contested.

The birth of a language cannot usually be dated, unless it is determined by political decision. For this, Afrikaans, whose one-hundredth birthday will soon be celebrated, is a good example. On 8 May 1925, a joint sitting of the House of Assembly and the Senate of the Union of South Africa passed the Official Languages of the Union Act which replaced Dutch by Afrikaans as one of the official languages of the Union. Earlier, in 1919, the Dutch Bible was translated into Afrikaans, which was seen as an important step towards languagehood. Language policy activities for further corpus planning followed. No longer looked down upon from the lectern of standard Dutch, what until then was known as *Kaaps Nederlands* (Cape Dutch) was thus officially elevated to language status. This was a success for the South African Academy for Science and

Arts that was founded in 1909 and includes the *Taalkommissie* (Language Commission) for *Nasionale Taalliggaam vir Afrikaans* (NTLA, National Language Body for Afrikaans) as one of its sections, which is still active today.[6]

Separation from Dutch did not much affect intercommunicability, since in excess of 90 per cent of its lexicon is of Dutch origin. However, pronunciation, words originating in other languages, notably Zulu, Xhosa, Twana, and some other African languages, as well as some grammatical changes, give it a distinct character. The legal act of recognition was followed by unceasing lexicographic and normative work on the part of the NTLA. Currently Afrikaans is one of the eleven official languages of South Africa, two of which, English and Afrikaans, are of European origin and nine are African languages. The language status of Afrikaans is undisputed; however, because of its association with segregationist Apartheid policies (1948 to early 1990s) and because the majority of its speakers are white and Coloured and only a small minority are Black, there is a racist subtext that casts a shadow over its future.

Purism

Racism is actually congenial with certain language ideologies, a very prominent one being linguistic purism. This is the idea that a language can exist and develop in isolation from others and ought to be protected against harmful outside influences, a concern most recently politicized by the Italian government, as pointed out at the beginning of this chapter. In Germany and Italy linguistic nationalism initially concentrated on society and state; deliberate language planning strategies were a subordinate and at times very difficult subject. By contrast, in Greece attention to language reform preceded the political drive for independence from the Ottoman Empire, under whose control it had been for more than three centuries.

After the Greek War of Independence from the multi-ethnic and multilingual Ottoman Empire in the 1820s, the language became a defining element of political sovereignty. In the spirit of the Romanticism of the time Greek was conceptualized as the embodiment of Greekness and the foundation of the national state. Initially, the population was anything but homogenous in terms of language and wouldn't be for many decades. In addition to speakers of Greek there were Slavs, Albanians, Ladino-speaking Jews, Vlachs, not to mention Turks and Turkish-speaking Greeks. In some regions, e.g., Salonica, Greek speakers were in the minority, and with every territorial expansion and every war in the nineteenth and early twentieth centuries refugees from Asia Minor and the Balkans who spoke various languages and dialects made for further diversification.

Against this background, intellectuals in Greece and in the diaspora developed an extensive discourse that politicized the Greek language. There was general accord about the importance of cultivating, teaching and thereby spreading the national language, but ideas as to what exactly this language should be differed widely, which led to long-lasting uncertainty, even chaos. In the final decades of the eighteenth century, scholar and humanist Adamantios Koraïs played a particularly influential role. Couched in Parisian diaspora and hence far away from the language people spoke in the streets of Greek cities, he dedicated himself to making the 'neglected Greek language' fit to serve the nation. This involved resorting to antiquated grammatical patterns and words. Taking sides with respect to Koraïs' proposals for a new Greek with old dignity, two factions emerged that loathed each other as if they were enemies of the nation. On one side stood conservative purists who were committed to the language of the cradle of European civilisation and promoted *Katharevousa*—literally 'the cleansed (language)', *katharo* meaning 'clean'—an antiquated literary variety that was supposed to connect its users to the language of Homer, Pericles, and Aristotle. Adamantios Koraïs had spearheaded its construction. It was a written language not spoken by anyone, but thought to give Greek the prestige it deserved. On the other side stood the Demoticists who were intent to streamline the vernacular of the common people, *Dimotikí*, regulate and standardize it so that it could unite the population, shape their social consciousness, and thus serve as the national language.

Both factions embraced linguistic nationalism wholeheartedly, but their corpus planning programmes pointed in opposite directions, and not just for a moment until a compromise line was found. This did not happen for over a century. Katharevousa promotors were determined that the vernacular, which had absorbed many foreign elements without much guidance for centuries, needed to be purified and debarbarized. Only a language with evident similarities to Ancient Greek could evoke the great Hellenistic legacy, which the Demoticists, in their view, were undermining. They were even accused of contaminating the Greek language with Slavic elements in order to bring Greece closer to Russia, and after the Russian Revolution, this charge was expanded to include labelling them as communists. In line with this kind of reasoning, Demoticists were also associated with atheism and an affront to the Greek Orthodox Church, which to most Greeks is conceptually as Greek as the language.

Meanwhile, the Katharevousists were said to cling to reactionary Hellenistic phantasies by promoting a dead language. If Greece was to become a modern state, its national language should be that of the people, which Katharevousists considered an insult to their ancient heritage. The split between the stylized language of public documents and formality and that of everyday communication—later considered a case of 'diglossia' in sociolinguistics (see p. 52)—thus continued. It was not until 1976 that the Demoticists prevailed when Demotic Greek was formally elevated to official and national status. Other language policy measures that followed included an orthography reform that did away with outdated polytonic diacritics that did not relate to anything in the spoken language. In spite of the fact that both parties wanted a renovated Greek national language, Demotic and Katharevousa proponents were extremely polarized ideologically.

The adoption in 1976 of Demotic Greek as the national and the official language of Greece has calmed the language conflicts that characterized the divided Greek speech community for so long, which, however does not mean that all controversial issues have been resolved. The purification of the Greek language is still on the agenda of many conservatives and gets official backing, notably by the Academy of Athens. One of its departments, the Research Centre for Scientific Terms and Neologisms founded in 1966, explains its purpose and mission as follows:

1. Linguistic inspection of the neologisms of the Modern Greek Language.
2. Suggestions for replacement of foreign neologisms with Greek terms—provided that the foreign neologisms have not yet been widely adopted—and for the proper use of the Greek language.
3. Formulation in Greek of recent scientific terminology in line with the new scientific achievements.[7]

Sacred legacy or promising future

Greek purism to some extent thrived on anti-Turkish sentiments. It is therefore ironic that a purist movement also emerged in post-Ottoman Turkey (Çolak 2004). In the event it was sponsored by the founding father of the Republic of Turkey and hence 'father of the Turks,'[8] Kemal Ataturk himself. Unlike Greek purism it did not initially refer to a glorious past long lost, but to a new culture for a new state. The language of rule of the Ottoman Empire, Ottoman Turkish or Osmanlıca, was written with a variety of the Arabic script and relied heavily on Arabic and Persian for religious and technical terminology. Ataturk and his associates found both incompatible with the pillars on which a modern Turkish nation state was to be based, secularism and nationalism.

The Turkish purists conceptualized their language as an artefact akin to French language policy ideas. The purist spirit that motivated the elimination of foreign elements from the language was tantamount to a break with the Islamic past. A purified Turkish, that was the idea, would help to promote westernization and modernization by freeing it from the outdated values encoded in Arabic and Persian words. By the same token, the Latin alphabet was an emblem of Western civilization and therefore opposed by traditionalists who considered it harmful to the unity of Islam. In 1928, a language commission was set up in Ankara to Latinize the writing system and write a new grammar of Turkish. In 1932, the Turkish Language Association (*Türk Dil Kurumu*)[9] was established as an official body charged with terminological innovation, especially replacing words of Arabic and Persian origin with ones that could pass as pure Turkish. A new, purified language was thus a central component of Turkey's modernization policy in the early twentieth century. In Kemal Ataturk's own words:

> A rich national language has great influence on the development of national feeling. The Turkish tongue is one of the richest of all; it only needs to be intelligently cultivated. The Turkish nation, which knows how to establish its government and its sublime independence, must also free its language from the yoke of foreign words (quoted from Çolak 2004: 75).

Purism is often a very conservative language ideology; however, as the example of early republican Turkey shows, emancipation from a past that is felt to stand in the way of progress and needed innovation can be an underlying motivation as well. The notion that a language could be pure is an illusion, but ideological beliefs, such as that Turkish is the 'mother of all languages', which gained popularity in the later stages of Turkey's purist movement, are rarely a matter of empirical verification. The Sun Language Theory (*Güneş Dil Teorisi*) which arose in the 1930s posited that human civilization began with the Alpine Brachycephalic race in Central Asia and all tongues were derived from a proto-Turkic language is an example of such ideological speculation. Language ideologies should not be made out of thin air because that may damage their credibility; however, like other belief systems, their acceptance depends as much on who promotes them as on the actual contents. More often than not they are intended to achieve a political goal rather than to prove the truth, even when they claim to be based on the truth.

Decolonization

Half a century after the decolonization of Africa largely came to an end, it is still common to refer to anglophone, francophone, and lusophone countries, although in virtually all cases only parts of the population are proficient in English, French, and Portuguese. 'X-speaking' refers to language status rather than speaker population.[10] To take the smallest group, in Angola, Cape Verde, Guinea-Bissau, Mozambique, São Tomé and Príncipe, and Equatorial Guinea Portuguese has the status of official language, as do French and English in 21 and 24 African countries respectively—with some overlap. These three European languages have taken root on the African continent, although the situations in which they exist today vary greatly. Portuguese is spoken by just 14 per cent of the population of Guinea-Bissau and almost the entire population of São Tomé and Príncipe, the biggest lusophone countries of the continent, Angola and Mozambique ranging in between at estimated 71 per cent and 50 per cent, respectively. A similarly broad range of proficiency levels of the populations is found in countries where French and English have (co-)official status (Table 3).

Table 3 Select examples of African countries where French and English have official status and the population share speaking these languages as L1 or L2[11]

French official	Population speaking L1 or L2 French	English official	Population speaking L1 or L2 English
Burundi (co-official with Kurundi and English)	9%	Tanzania	15%
Senegal	26%	Zambia	18%
Central African Republic	29%	Cameroon	20%
Togo	41%	South Africa	41%
Gabon	65%	Ghana	66%

In Africa, French and English, like Portuguese, exist in multilingual environments virtually everywhere and despite their official status are regularly used by parts of the population only. There is one country, Equatorial Guinea, where alongside French and Portuguese Spanish has official status and is spoken by 70 per cent of the population. Some 15 Indigenous languages are also spoken in this small country with a population of just a little more than 1.5 million (2023). The multilingualism found here seems extreme, but in the African context it is not. If we take the generally recognized number of languages spoken in Africa, which ranges around 2000, they outnumber that of sovereign states by a factor of 37 or so, which implies among other things that patterns of communication between government and citizen do not and cannot conform with the ideology of one state one language and a linguistically homogenized population. This is the main reason why the terminology of 'lusophone, anglophone, and francophone countries' has become the target of criticism in theories of intellectual decolonization (Makoni, Severo and Abdelhay 2023). Far from being pragmatic labels for the sake of brevity, these terms reflect and perpetuate European language ideologies such as monolingualism, linguistic nationalism, and purism. They ignore the linguistic reality of the respective countries both with respect to the multitude of languages and localized varieties of the colonial languages. Rather than being divided in neatly separated compartments, the linguistic scene of Africa must be conceived as continuously changing, which is hard to conciliate with the worldview of national languages. This is why the linguistic legacy of colonialism is nowhere more problematic than in Africa. Consider the example of Mozambique.

Mozambique gained independence in 1975. According to Lopes (2004), Portuguese was then the official language of the country as a matter of course and the only language of instruction from elementary first grade onward. In 1990, this language policy was reconfirmed in Article 5 of the revised constitution, which at the same time emphasized the importance of the more than 40 Indigenous languages.[12] This was largely a symbolic gesture, but it opened the door for new language policy initiatives, in education in particular but also more broadly. In line with UNESCO's repeated recommendations[13] to use pupils' mother language as medium of instruction, bilingual education is now officially supported and several such experimental programmes have been introduced over the past decades. Implementing these programmes has not been easy, as not all parents or teachers are convinced of the merits of this kind of education. Although many teachers recognize the advantages of bilingualism in theory, in practice they prefer to shift to teaching in Portuguese at an early stage, as it is the official language of national examinations (Terra 2021). Dealing with a multitude of languages in an educational system that is designed to produce equitable results is a challenge which is compounded by other factors, notably the increasing diversity of urban centres brought about by internal migration. Yet another dynamic that characterizes Portuguese in Mozambique, as it does English in anglophone countries, is the advance of Africanized varieties of the colonial national languages. These varieties and the high esteem they often enjoy among their users again testify to language attitudes and conceptions that deviate from normative European patterns.

In Kenya and Uganda, to cite two 'English speaking' countries of Africa, domestic migration and the diversification of urban environments that gives rise to new hybrid varieties of English also pose problems for the official bilingual education policy. Schools are required to use a/the dominant local language as the language of learning for the first three years and then switch to English as medium of instruction. Empirical studies in Kenya suggest that using English as a medium of instruction in elementary school is detrimental to quality education results (Sibomana 2015). On the basis of interviews and empirical testing, Ssentanda (2019) arrived at similar findings in Uganda. The established language-in-education policy of shifting to English as medium of instruction after three years of using local languages had much better results in private schools than in government schools and pupils of very linguistically diverse areas were left behind. 'Uganda needs to rethink how English is taught in rural contexts' (ibid.), she concluded.

Such findings paired with somewhat contradictory attitudes towards their official languages can be found in the school systems of many African countries and must be considered a colonial relic. Liberation from colonial rule was much desired and local cultures, traditions, and languages must be honoured, but the languages of the former colonizers are still attractive, as they provide access to a larger world and to economic opportunities that local languages do not offer. It is not surprising that in the age of the commercialization of everything this weighs heavily, making it difficult to align language-in-education policies with developments on the ground. Language attitudes are perhaps the most convincing proof that the wheel of history cannot be turned back, which makes language policy an important subject of post-colonial theory (Makoni, Severo and Abdelhay 2023).

*

To sum up, language ideologies are highly complex conceptual systems that reflect the instrumentalization of language for various purposes, the relationship between different speech communities, as well as the interaction of language and other artefacts, notably nation, religion, and race. A key property of European language ideologies is to mark dividing lines of inclusion and exclusion. As the examples of Greece (*Katharevousa*), Turkey (*öz Türkçe*), Catalan, and Afrikaans have shown, linguistic nationalism, purism, and linguistic separatism are prominent language ideologies that can be observed not only in the countries discussed above. They came into being in train with European modernization and were taken and adjusted to other parts of the world. The post-colonial perspective, briefly touched upon in the final section of this chapter, reveals that language ideologies can be far removed from reality and yet exercise a long-lasting influence on both language policies and popular language attitudes.

A prime topic of language ideology, so far touched upon only in passing, is linguistic authority. Who is entitled or commissioned to research, establish, and explain the rules of a regulated language, and has the right to direct language choices within existing grammar and vocabulary conventions in specific directions that are binding for official use, education, and media? It is to this question that we now turn.

Further reading

Fichte, Johann Gottlieb. 1922 [1807/08]. *Reden an die Deutsche Nation*. English translation by R.F. Jones and G.R. Turnbull, *Addresses to the German Nation*. Chicago and London: The Open Court Publishing Co. Internet Archive: https://ia800201.us.archive.org/9/items/addressestogerma00fich/addressestogerma00fich.pdf

Kritikos, Georgios. 2013. The nationalism of Greek language: the two faces of Janus in the early twentieth century. *Balkan Studies* 47: 133–163. https://www.imxa.gr/files/bsfiles/47/Kritikos.pdf

Lüpke, Friederike & Anne Storch (eds.) 2013. *Repertoires and Choices in African languages*. Berlin, New York: Walter de Gruyter.

Mazzini, Giuseppe. 2005 [1860]. *The Duties of Man and other Essays*. New York: Cosimo.

Woolard, Kathryn A. 2020. Language ideology. In James Stanlaw (ed.) *The International Encyclopedia of Linguistic Anthropology*. https://doi.org/10.1002/9781118786093.iela0217

6

Agents of language policy

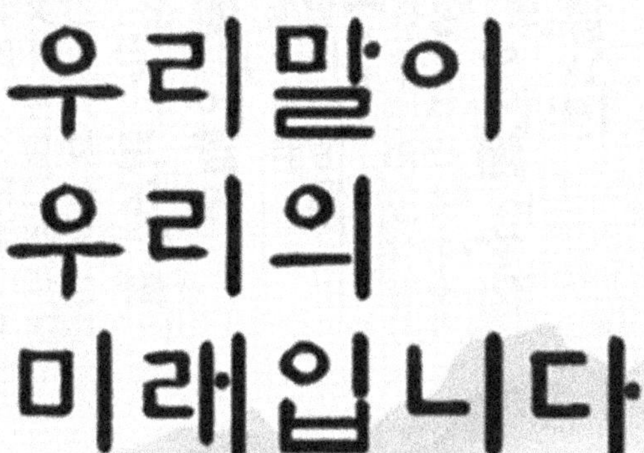

Uliui eon-eoneum uliui milaei bnida

'Our language is our future'

Mission of the National Institute of Korean Language, Republic of Korea

To develop Korean language and to improve Korean language-life of the people

Conducting researches for Korean language policies

Increasing language-life convenience through supplementing linguistic standards

Language Policy. Florian Coulmas, Oxford University Press. © Florian Coulmas (2025).
DOI: 10.1093/9780191976377.003.0006

Improving the environment of using the Korean language for smooth communication

Building a foundation for a qualitative improvement of the Korean language education

Collecting national language resources and reinforcing the integrated information service[1]

Language regulators: what they are

For the implementation of language policies various institutions have been created, including many language academies. Nowadays such language regulator bodies outnumber sovereign states, reflecting the fact that not only national languages are the subject of research, regulation, and promotion. Still, language regulators only deal with languages that enjoy some kind of official recognition. With their activities they have contributed to increasing inequality of the languages of the world, for thanks to them a small minority of all languages are carefully studied, recorded, normalized, and ideologized, as discussed in the previous chapter, while most other languages exist without administrative scaffold and philosophical superstructure.

Language academies are part of the modern world where linguistic meaning shifts ever more from the intentional—tied to the speaker: what they mean—to the conventional: what it, the word, means—preserved in the dictionary for everyone's reference. Even though the overarching purposes and specific tasks of language academies differ from each other, they all assume that authority over language, setting standards, enacting rules, and developing lexical resources and teaching materials, are possible and desirable. Looking back over a history of several hundred years, there can be little doubt that language academies, and through them language policies, had an impact on the linguistic configuration of the world. Since they serve very different sized language communities, it goes without saying that their impact varies in strength.

The effect of the Academy of the Dhivehi Language, established in 2011 and tasked with promoting the Dhivehi language of the Maldives, will be all but invisible, while that of the Académie française, founded in 1635 and today perhaps the most famous of all language academies, is considerable. Assessing the influence of such institutions is difficult; however, if they have any effect at all, it is obvious that the mere size of the respective language communities, 300,000 of Dhivehi vs. 300 million of French, makes for a huge difference.

If we order the language academies by size of language community, the top ten will be Chinese, Hindi, Arabic, Spanish, French, Bengali, Russian, Portuguese, Urdu, and Indonesian (Table 4). Conspicuously absent from this list is the most widely spoken (first, second, foreign combined) language of the world, English. It is not on the list because an English language regulatory body has never been established in Britain or elsewhere. The British Council is an organization designed, in its own words, to 'promote cultural relationships between the people of the United Kingdom and other countries; develop a wider knowledge of the English language; and encourage educational co-operation between the United Kingdom and other countries.'[2] Developing a wider knowledge of English in the world is a language policy goal, however, unlike the institutions listed in Table 4, the tasks of the British Council never included the regulation, standardization, or reform of the English language.

Table 4 Language regulation institutions of populous language communities

Language	Year established	Title	Associated with
Chinese	1928 1949 2007	National Language Committee, Taiwan (dissolved 2013) National Language and Writing Committee* Research Centre for the Collection and Regulation of Written Chinese	Promote Mandarin Council, Singapore 1979; Chinese Language Standardization Council of Malaysia, 1997

Continued

Table 4 *Continued*

Language	Year established	Title	Associated with
Hindi	1960	Central Hindi Directorate	
(Modern Standard) Arabic	1919	Arab Academy of Damascus	13 Arabic language academies in other countries
Spanish	1713	Royal Spanish Academy	23 Spanish language academies in other countries
French	1635	Académie Française	
Bengali	1955	Bangla Academy, Bangladesh	Paschimbanga Bangla Academy, Kolkata, India, since 1986
Russian	1783 1944 2015	Imperial Russian Academy V.V. Vinogradov Russian Language Institute of the Russian Academy of Sciences Concept for State Support and Promotion of the Russian Language	
Portuguese	1779	Lisbon Science Academy, Class of Letters	Academia Brasileira de Letras, since 1897
Urdu	1979	National Language Promotion Department, Pakistan	National Council for Promotion of Urdu Language, India, since 1996
Indonesian	1947/1948	Language Development and Fostering Agency	

*Guójiā yŭyán wénzì gōngzuò wěiyuánhuì (国家语言文字工作委员会) was in 1998 integrated in China's Ministry of Education and became part of the Department of Language and Writing Information Management.[3]

If we add the speakers of English and the next nine most numerous languages to those represented in Table 4, we arrive in demographic terms at close to 75 per cent of the world population. In other words, 0.28 per cent of all languages—20 of some 7000—account for close to 75 per cent of the world population. Because of the difficulties of counting languages and distinguishing between first and second language speakers in such statistics, this is no more than a rough number to illustrate the inverse relation between the number of languages and that of their speakers: there are few languages with many speakers and many languages with few speakers. Statistically, 80 per cent of all languages are spoken by fewer than 100,000 people. It is by and large the big languages for which regulator institutions have been created, the Italian Accademia della Crusca, founded in 1583 and not included in the table because Italian is not among the top ten or even twenty most populous languages of the world, having been the model for others that were established in the course of the European Renaissance and Enlightenment. The pathos of the maxims of some of these agencies reminds us of the great importance then attached to the development of languages.

Accademia della Crusca: *Il più bel fior ne coglie* (It [the academy] gathers the most beautiful flowers)
Académie Française: *à l'immortalité* (to immortality)
Real Academia Española: *Limpia, fija y esplendor* (purified, fastened and dignified)
Academia das Ciências de Lisboa: *Nisi utile est quod facimus stulta est gloria* (in Latin: There is no glory unless what we do is useful.)
Academia Brasileira de Letras (*1897), echoing the Académie française: *ad immortalitatem.*
Central Hindi Directorate: *I am the one who gives wealth to the nation*[4]
Lia Rumanscha: *Tranter Rumantschs be rumantsch* (Among Romans only Romansh)

Some academies for small languages such as Dhivehi, Greenlandic, and Romansh exist, but these only came into being in the twentieth century. Language academies belong to modernity and in many ways belong to the nation state. Since modernity was pioneered in Europe and the concept of the nation state was born there together with the development of capitalism and state-mandated education, the first such institutions were established in Europe. Whether, and if so how, they influenced the diffusion of European languages around the world in train with colonialism is a question yet unanswered. That power, regardless of any academic backing, plays a major role in language spread is well known, and the spread of English in particular suggests that a general answer to this question will not be easy to find.

Many language academies are national institutions dedicated to the observation and administration of the national language or, as in the case of Bahasa Indonesia discussed in Chapter 5, to elevating a language to national status. The Westphalian system notwithstanding, coincidence of linguistic and political boundaries always has been the exception rather than the rule, as it still is. It is, therefore, quite common for a language academy's actions to directly or indirectly affect not all citizens of its country, or, conversely, citizens from more than one country. Enumerating all language academies goes beyond the scope of this chapter. Suffice it, therefore, to distinguish the most common and important configurations:

One regulatory agency for the national language of one country. The Centre for the Greek Language, which is involved in both corpus and status planning of the Greek language, and the Academy of Athens which includes research centres dealing with modern Greek dialects and investigating and recommending for use terminology and neologism, function in this manner.[5] Another example is the Icelandic Language Institute, which was created in 1985 and reports to the Ministry of Education, Science, and Culture of Iceland.

One regulatory agency for a national language that is also spoken in other countries is, for example, the Dutch Taalunie.[6] It brings together members from the Kingdom of the Netherlands including the overseas territories Aruba, Curaçao and Sint Maarten, the Dutch-speaking region of the Kingdom of Belgium, Flanders, and, since 2004, the Republic of Suriname. The Taalunie is an intergovernmental organization, which means that all activities it undertakes are carried out in collaboration with the three governments.

One regulatory agency for one minority language in one country. The Lia Rumantscha[7] established in 1919 as an organization that promotes the study, normalization, and usage of Romansh in Switzerland.

Two regulating agencies for one language that is the national language of one country and a minority language in another, as for instance Urdu in Pakistan and India, respectively. Where political relations between countries are tense, as in this case, collaboration between language regulators on both sides can be difficult.

By contrast, the Malay language is subject to regulation in Malaysia, Brunei, and Singapore where the Institute of Language and Literature in Kuala Lumpur, the Language and Literature Bureau in Bandar Seri Begawan, and the Malay Language Council, Singapore, respectively cooperate.

Two (or more) regulatory agencies for a language that is a minority language wherever it is spoken, such as Berber (Amazigh). In this case, both the Algerian Academy of the Amazigh Language and the Moroccan *Institut royal de la culture amazighe* take issue with maintaining and developing the Berber language, and to some extent cooperate.

One country with regulating agencies for more than one of its languages. In India, multilingualism has a quality of its own inasmuch as the country, which is projected to become the most populous country in the world by the end of the decade, is home to a great many languages with long literary traditions and official status that are not considered minority languages in the states where they are spoken. Accordingly, India has regulating agencies not only for its official language, Hindi, so stipulated in Article 343 of its constitution, but also for Urdu, Bengali, Marathi, Tamil, Telugu, among others.

One regulating agency of a former colonial power that left its language behind in several countries is prototypically exemplified by the Académie française, which is still respected in many African countries as a relevant norm-setting agency. As discussed in Chapter 5, language is an enduring legacy of colonialism. The long shadow cast by colonial language regimes to this day is also illustrated by the Royal Spanish Academy's collaboration with 23 other language academies indicated in Table 4.

Two (or more) national agencies charged with regulating the same language, as for instance, Korean by the North Korean Centre of the Social Science Institute and the Korean Language Policy Bureau in the South Korean Ministry of Culture, Sports, and Tourism whose mission statement is cited at the outset of this chapter. In addition, there is the China Korean Language Regulatory Commission that oversees Korean language education for some 2 million ethnic Koreans in China.

These examples illustrate, but do not exhaust, the variety of sociolinguistic and political environments in which language regulating organizations are placed and with which they must contend. Due to the incongruency of state populations and language communities, these situations involve majority-minority relations, written and unwritten languages, literate and oral/pre-literate population groups, socially stratified language varieties, classical and liturgical languages, among others. At the same time, language academies and other regulator organizations vary with regard to forms of incorporation, structure, budget, and staff, but they all affirm the fact that in the modern world language is an object of state responsibility and hence political relevance. The scope of this responsibility also varies, reflecting historical, sociolinguistic, and geopolitical circumstances, as well as political traditions and preferences. What then are the principal tasks of language regulators?

Language regulators: what they do

First of all, language regulation is about written languages, and so is language policy, including when it is about giving an unwritten language a written form. Providing a language with a writing system is a task with two aspects that characterize language policy more generally, scholarship and politics. Since politics always and consciously follows an ideological path, but scholarship at least attempts to approach its object of investigation impartially, there is a tension between the two. Separating or unifying linguistic varieties—Afrikaans vs. Dutch, Luxembourgish vs. German, Galician vs. Portuguese, Karelian vs. Finnish, Isan vs. Thai—often is a political as much as a linguistic matter which implies that linguists who are employed to justify one or the other solution have to work for a stated goal rather than to find a well-founded answer to the question. This is a tension that also characterizes work on other language policy projects. In recognition of the competence of specialists, language academies rely on trained linguists and philologists. However, in addition to being a potential object of research, every language is a means of communication and, as the case may be, a cherished symbol of belonging, which is why non-specialists may claim as much authority about their language as professionals. In this field of tension, whether language academies consider themselves more as scientific or political organizations depends on the tasks they have set themselves or have been prescribed by law.

Paradigmatically, among the 40 *immortels*, as the members of the Académie française are known, one finds over the decades and centuries politicians, diplomates, civil servants, philosophers, novelists, poets, lawyers, journalists, natural scientists, medical doctors, and soldiers, but philologists and linguists are few and far between. Given such a membership, the stated objective of the academy is less surprising than one would expect when thinking about an organization dealing with language. The first subtitle of its lengthy mission statement identifies the task of the academy in no uncertain terms: 'the defence of the French language'. The French language, it suggests, is under attack and therefore needs an institution to defend it. The language thus becomes a metaphor of the nation. Since the name of the academy is ambiguous and could mean academy of France or academy of the French language, this is actually not far-fetched, but the wording raises the question of who or what the language must be defended against.

The threats of course change with time, but the defence must be at the ready and the order of command is clear, as emerges from another passage from the mission statement: 'The French Academy was therefore created in 1635, to give official weight to the work of grammarians.'[8] The grammarians did the drudgery; the immortals sanctioned it and harvested the glory. In the early years after the Académie had been founded, defence walls had to be erected against regionalisms, archaisms, and deviations, and rather than being derived from observing how people speak, 'precise rules had to be *given* to the language in order to make it pure, eloquent and capable to deal with the arts and sciences,' as stated in Art. 24 of the Statutes. The members of the academy, each in their specialty, contributed by their work to confer prestige on the language, which could thus become an instrument of power and diplomacy. And the martial allegory is still in place. The year 2014 was dedicated by the Academy to the 'reconquête de la langue française'. Nowadays, it is no longer the dignity of Latin, grammatical uncertainty, or regionalisms from Picard and Breton that threaten the standing of French. They have been replaced by *marketing, managers, emails, chatter, brainstorming, digital, jogging, burn-out* and thousands of Anglo-Saxon loanwords as well as pseudo-Anglicisms, such as *updater* and *customiser* that for the past several decades have formed the *péril anglaise.* French needs to be reconquered from the anglicization of its dictionary, a battle too great to be fought by the academy alone. The Ministry of Culture and Communication, therefore, in 1996 established the *Commission Générale de terminologie et de néologie*, which under the supervision of the academy would coin new French words to resist and win back territory swamped by English terms in all-important spheres of contemporary life, not to mention gender-neutral diction, a frontline to which we will return in Chapter 11.

French did rise to become the universal language of diplomacy, unrivalled for some time in the nineteenth and early twentieth century. Was this at least in part due to the academy's work? The fact that after the peace treaty negotiations of Versailles and more so after World War II, on the international scene French was gradually being pushed aside by another language of power, no matter what the academy did to defend it, suggests that the influence of a language regulator organization is limited, even if it is as well-equipped as the Académie française. Status (officialization), corpus (dictionary and grammar), and prestige can be planned and implemented with desired and unexpected effects; and then there is real power, military, economic, and political, which inevitably interferes with what language policies can achieve. This is not to say it's negligible, but it always has to be seen in context.

Other than the grand ideological missions, what are the most important activities of language regulating organizations? In attempting to answer this question, the remainder of this chapter will look at three areas of activity: writing and script reform, lexicology and terminology, and language spread.

Writing reform

China prides itself of one of the oldest writing systems and the longest unbroken literary heritage of the world. When the Chinese Character Reform Association (*Zhōngguó wénzì gǎigé xiéhuì*) was established on the same day or shortly after the founding of the People's Republic of China, 10 October 1949, it was a major event indicative of the importance the new government attached to language policy matters. It considered writing reform necessary based on a simple and intuitive assumption.[9] The Chinese writing system which consists of thousands of complex characters is demanding to learn. Despite China's grand literary tradition, the literacy rate of the population was low compared to more advanced countries, estimated between only 15 to 25 per cent. There had to be a causal relationship, or that was the assumption. In order to raise literacy levels and promote education, China's written language had to be reformed. Specific goals quickly emerged that such a reform had to achieve: the standardization of modern Chinese, character simplification and, even more radically, Romanization. All powerful nations used alphabetic writing, Mao Zedong himself observed, so China, too, should move in that direction.[10] That many alphabetic systems (English among them) are anything but simple or phonetic did not enter the discussion of the Committee of the Reform of the Chinese Written Language, which in 1954 succeeded the above-mentioned association.

Work on standardization and an alphabetic writing system and spelling proceeded succinctly. A character simplification scheme was submitted to and formally approved by the State Council in 1956. The reform reduced the graphic complexity of many characters by lessening the number of consisting strokes which, the reformers argued, should make learning them easier (Table 5).

Table 5 Traditional and simplified Chinese characters

Traditional characters	弗洛裏安·庫爾馬斯
Simplified characters	弗洛里安·库尔马斯
Romanization (*hànyǔ pīnyīn*)	Fú luò lǐ ān·kù ěr mǎ sī

As the example illustrates, some characters have not changed at all, the first, second, fourth, and eighth, while the equivalence of others, such as the sixth, is hard to recognize. The overall rate of strokes per character in the example is reduced from 9.6 to 8.0. Does this make learning easier? Irrefutable evidence in support of this argument has never been produced, but the reform scheme was implemented and is today the basis of writing Chinese in China. That literacy rates in Taiwan and Japan were for many years higher than in China in spite of traditional characters being used there suggests that other factors of pedagogy and the school system have a stronger influence on educational achievements and literacy levels.

Originally conceived as the ultimate goal of the reform, Romanization never materialized. In any case it did not replace Chinese characters, the reasons for holding on to the traditional script being too weighty. However, a Chinese Romanization scheme, *Hànyǔ pīnyīn*, (hereafter *Pinyin*) for a standardized common language, *Pǔtōnghuà*, 'common language', widely called *Mandarin*, was successfully created and today fulfils important functions for reference and linguistic unification, both across Chinese dialects and for the 55 recognized ethnic minorities, as its country-wide promotion continues.[11]

An order of the president of the PRC of October 2000 states that '[t]he language work department of the State Council is responsible for planning, guiding, managing and supervising the work of the national standard spoken and written language'. It further stipulates that 'the language work department of the State Council promulgates the standard of Putonghua proficiency tests'. To secure the implementation of these and some other provisions it instructs that 'those who violate the provisions of this law and interfere with others' learning and use of the national standard spoken and written language shall be ordered by the relevant administrative departments to make corrections within a time limit and given a warning'.[12] With a population of 1.425 billion people (2023), implementing a standard is a permanent endeavour rather than a task that can be shelved once completed.

One effect of the character simplification scheme, worth mentioning here because similar political by-products often accompany writing reforms, was that simplified characters became a symbol of communist China and were therefore disparaged in Taiwan and Hong Kong. The substantive merits or defects of the reform had nothing to do with this rejection. Writing systems, scripts, and orthographies are linked to cultural traditions and, therefore, ideologically charged, which becomes clear whenever reforms are proposed and implemented. Visibility affords writing symbolic qualities that are easily put at the service of political disputes.

Discussions about writing reform proposals seem to focus mostly on systematic and procedural aspects on the surface, but underneath there often is a subcurrent of less scientific arguments such as 'we despise you/your policies', 'change corrupts our glorious heritage', etc. Writing reforms remind us of something we tend to forget. Being socialized into a literate society, there is no choice as to how we write. The school and the primer admit of no deviation. The norm is set. But when a reform is proposed choice is inescapable, which usually means that it will be politicized. The distribution of writing systems around the world is clear testimony to ideological and political influence. Religion is perhaps the most powerful factor: Latin: Roman Catholicism and Protestantism; Cyrillic: Eastern Orthodoxy; Arabic: Islam; Brahmi (derived): Hinduism; Chinese: Buddhism, Confucianism. Colonial legacy is another factor, as well illustrated by two spelling conventions for the Malay language using the Latin alphabet. As mentioned above, in British Malaya, the spelling was modelled on English, in the Netherlands East Indies on Dutch, which often obscures lexical identity. The Malay word for 'grandchild', for instance, is spelt *chuchu* in Malaysia and *tjoetjoe* in Indonesia, but both are pronounced the same.

Ease of transfer from one language to another, English to Malay and Dutch to Malay/Indonesian, respectively, is a more important motive of choice of spelling convention than any language-internal reasons. Kazakh is another instructive example. A Turkic language of Central Asia, it has been and is written in three alphabets within a mere century. Under the influence of the Islamic Ottoman Empire, the Kazakh language adopted a great many loan words from Arabic and Persian and used the Arabic consonant alphabet. After the Russian Revolution, when Kazakhstan became an Autonomous Socialist Soviet Republic first and then a full union republic, the government in Moscow initially supported Romanization as a means of detaching the population from Islam and uniting all ethnolinguistic groups of the union. Before long, however, Cyrillic was favoured as the alphabet that would, if not unite, at least link all the Indigenous language groups. The dissolution of the Soviet Union then prompted another turnaround.

The 1999 Constitution of the Republic of Kazakhstan provided for several legal acts regarding the use and development of the Kazakh languages, which was declared the state language, while Russian maintained co-official status. In 2017, the Kazakh government ordered a new Latin Kazakh alphabet to be created and implemented.[13] Not surprisingly, this did not lead to the unification of written Kazakh, which nowadays uses Latin and Cyrillic in Kazakhstan and Mongolia, while the Kazakh-speaking minority in China continues to use an Arabic-derived consonant alphabet.

Along the way of this zigzag, the linguistic advantages of the three systems, their linguistic fit, the use of diacritics such as umlauts and cedillas, etc., have been hotly debated, but the sobering bottom line is that these arguments are overshadowed by affective and political ones.

The general lesson to be drawn from the three cases above is that it is important, even indispensable in modern society, for written communication to have a standard, but it does not matter much what it is like. An effective school system can compensate for systematic flaws of the writing system to be imparted on pupils in elementary school. To substantiate this assertion with yet another example, Japan is in pole position in the race to have the world's most convoluted writing system, but has a good school system that puts it at the forefront of international educational achievement tests such as PISA.

Terminology policies

As the world and our societies change, so do our languages, which we are made most aware of through new words. Lexical innovation is constant, as in our daily experience we deal with new situations we wish to communicate about, and as scientific discoveries and technical inventions need to be articulated, not to mention fashion and social trends. Just think of 'doxxing' or 'allyship' or 'anti-vaxer', 'asymptomatic', 'herd immunity', 'lockdown', 'superspreader', and many other words that have been coined or revitalised[14] and spread together with the Covid-19 pandemic, a new experience for most people in most countries. The need for neologisms can be met in two ways: let things take their course and leave it to the language community, or commission experts to do the work. Two clear cases in this respect are English and Latin. There is no tradition in English and no language regulating institution in the Anglo-Saxon world that takes care of this kind of work. Moreover, the language community is so large and socially and geographically widespread that no explicit instructions for new word formation seem necessary.

By contrast, the language community of Latin is small, includes no native speakers and has little or no contact with everyday life. Yet there is an interested group of speakers who want to be able to use Latin for expressing contemporary contents. Mainly housed in the Vatican, they rely on experts to keep Latin lexically up to date. Article 2 of the Statutes of the Pontifical Academy for Latin identifies as one of its aims 'to promote the use of Latin in various contexts, both as a written and as a spoken language'.[15] In other words, rather than gather dust as a liturgical language Latin should stay fit for current communications, including *tuus adventus in paginam publicam Papae Francisci*[16] at @Pontifex_pt.[17] For the terminological and lexical updating of Latin, the Pontifical Academy relies on experts charged with compiling a *Lexicon recentis latinitatis* containing entries on public life, science, technology, religion, medicine, politics, and sports. Thanks to their efforts, you can now inform your friends in Latin that *meum instrumentum computatorium est detruncate* (my computer was hacked) and about many other pedestrian and highbrow subjects. We see here quite a bit of recycling because so much of English and other European languages' technical terminology is based on a Latin (and Greek) lexical layer.

Lexical recycling in the service of new vocabulary formation can be observed wherever a classical language, that is, one with an ancient body of literature, is available, such as Ancient Greek, Classical Chinese, Vedic Sanskrit, Classical Persian, Quranic Arabic, among others. For language academies, these languages are important resources for creating new words and technical terms. The extent to which these resources are exploited deliberately rather than spontaneously as in English depends to some extent on policy guidelines. Hindi in India is a case in point.

Established a good decade after the end of British rule in India, the Central Hindi Directorate in the Ministry of Education is, in its own words, 'the topmost institution in the country associated with the noble cause of development of Hindi'.[18] The main tasks of the directorate are the development of the Hindi language, compiling monolingual and bi- and multilingual dictionaries of Hindi and with other languages of

India, organize Hindi language courses, and develop educational materials. Instructions for the lexical development of the language order to secure the 'enrichment of Hindi by assimilating without interfering with its genius, the forms, style and expressions used in Hindustani and in other languages of India specified in the eighth schedule[19] and by drawing, wherever necessary or desirable, for its vocabulary, primarily on Sanskrit and secondarily on other languages'.[20] Hindustani is a compromise language between Hindi and Urdu which pre-independence political activists, notably Jawaharlal Nehru and Mahatma Gandhi, wanted to become the national language of India. Gandhi opined that

> There is no difference between Hindi and Urdu. Written in Devanagari, it is Hindi; the same written in Arabic script becomes Urdu. Those writers and speakers who deliberately use Sanskrit or Arabic and Persian words, do great harm to the country.[21]

The project to merge Urdu and Hindi into one language fell victim to the Partition of India, which made Hindi and Urdu move further away from each other. The former is made to draw 'primarily on Sanskrit', while the latter cultivates its Perso-Arabic lexical heritage. What appears to be a technical issue of terminology is actually part of the unresolved political question of the status of Hindi in India.

Since independence, Hindi supporters have lobbied for its spread across the country and its establishment as the national language. In non-Hindi speaking states in the south of the country this always met with resistance and still does, witness the tragic incident reported at the beginning of Chapter 2. As I was writing this chapter, the Indian government under Prime Minister Narendra Modi started a campaign, directed against the 'colonial relic' English, to make Hindi compulsory in education, even at the university level to offer for the first time ever medical degrees in Hindi. This push for Hindi provoked severe reactions from both academics and politicians. The finance minister of Tamil Nadu Palanivel Thiaga Rajan, for example, called the recommendations 'comprehensively unacceptable [. . .] profoundly wrong, regressive and retarding'.[22] And surgeon Dr Rajan Sharma, Hindi speaker and former head of the Indian Medical Council, deplored the ideological motivation behind the decision which he called 'regressive, backward-looking, pathetic and deplorable'.[23] The strategy of resorting to Sanskrit for terminology development, and Modi's language policy in general, is driven by the desire to overcome the 'colonial mindset', which critics of colonialism will not find difficult to understand. However, this policy is oblivious to the fact that the past cannot be changed and that the reasons for using English in scholarship are today not the same as they were in colonial times. This must be admitted, although colonialism has greatly contributed to the status English enjoys today, which has been characterized as the result of 'linguistic imperialism', a notion popularized above all by Robert Phillipson (1992). Many discussions over the past 30 years have underpinned the justification of this term, but this has not weakened the position of English in India or elsewhere. What is more, in non-Hindi speaking states English is preferred as overarching link language because it is more neutral than Hindi.

Looking at terminology formation from a global perspective, which in the digital age is hardly eccentric, words compete with each other, but it is never an unbiased competition in a free market. It is shaped by national language policy directives, purism, anti-language X–ism and other ideologies, tradition, school curricula, language contact chains, and the power positions of the countries behind the languages involved. Typological and structural features that make it easier to borrow from one language than from another also play a role, and of course power. It is no coincidence that today the main language of the greatest military power is the largest donor language from which technical terms and other words are integrated into other languages around the globe. Also, the trade balance of loanwords between neighbouring languages is never even, simply because there is a power differential between the language communities and their languages. The motivations of the French 'reconquest of terminology territory occupied by English' and the reactivation of Sanskrit for lexical innovation by Hindi proponents in India go beyond technical issues of corpus planning, standardization, and documentation. They are part of a national terminology policy.

In the knowledge society, a terminology policy formulated at the level of political decision making is of great importance, concerning as it does thousands of new terms annually that must be integrated into textbooks for schools and universities and recommended to public and private research institutes. In many countries, developing and implementing terminology policy belong to tasks of language regulator organizations. In order not to fall behind as new fields of knowledge and communication develop, and not to see their languages becoming unusable for these purposes, smaller language communities in particular devote great attention to terminology, which is also why UNESCO offers guidelines for terminology policy.[24]

Language dissemination policies

The third area in which academies and other language regulators are active is language dissemination, a notion that remains neutral in relation to whether languages are offered or imposed thereby. Some examples with numbers provided by the agencies themselves:

L'Alliance française is a government-financed agency that maintains some 800 language centres attended by more than 500,000 students in 136 countries.

The British Council is a registered charity that collaborates with some 200 countries and territories and is present in more than 100 countries. In 2021–2022 it reached 650 million people.

The *Instituto Camões Portugal* is dedicated to the worldwide promotion of the Portuguese language, culture, and values with Portuguese Language Centres in some 30 countries on five continents.

The *Società Dante Alighieri* is a non-profit association dedicated to the promotion, protection and dissemination of the Italian language and culture in the world. In online, hybrid, and face-to-face classrooms, 29 offices in 29 countries and five schools in Italy, it reaches out to students around the world.

The *Goethe Institut* was established in 1951 in the Federal Republic of Germany. It is a registered charity that operates on a legally independent basis and today has 158 seats in 98 countries. It supports 100,000 schools worldwide in giving German language tuition where more than half a million people sit a German language exam annually.

The *Instituto Cervantes* is a non-profit organization established by the Spanish government in 1991, which has 88 centres in 45 countries dedicated above all to the international promotion of Spanish as a second language.

The Swedish Academy is a cultural institution, founded in 1786 by King Gustaf III in order to advance the Swedish language and Swedish literature. The academy's main objective is to work for the 'purity, vigour, and majesty' of the Swedish language, i.e., its clarity, expressiveness, and prestige.

The *Pontificia Academia Latinitatis* was established in 2012 for the promotion and appreciation of the Latin language and culture. Its aim is to promote the use of Latin in various contexts, both as a written and as a spoken language.

The Japan Foundation, established in October 1972, as a special legal entity supervised by the Ministry of Foreign Affairs with a global network of 25 overseas offices in 24 countries. One of its purposes is to create and enhance Japanese-language education environments in order to give more people around the world opportunities to study Japanese.

The Confucius Institute, founded in 2004, is a cultural promotion organization under the Ministry of Education of the People's Republic of China. Today it includes more than 500 institutes of various legal forms around the world. To promote Chinese through innovative approaches to foreign language education (new media, social networks, virtual worlds, and gaming) is one of its stated purposes.

Eight of the ten examples above are organizations dedicated to the dissemination of European languages. This is not an arbitrary choice, but a representative selection, for deliberate language promotion policies evolved following their dissemination in the age of colonialism. How contexts change is particularly noticeable in the post-colonial world. Colonial languages, especially Spanish, Portuguese, French, English, and Dutch have changed the linguistic map of the world, and we are witnessing changes again in the post-colonial era, some of which relate directly to language regulating organizations. It is also worth noting, although perhaps obvious, that language dissemination policies and organizations are maintained by rich countries. They can afford such policies and their languages are economically attractive, as we will discuss in more detail in Chapter 8.

The other two examples confirm this relationship. While in pre-modern times few European intellectuals would have studied Chinese and even fewer Japanese, a politically motivated and supported policy of disseminating these two languages was beyond imagination. It was only when gross national product and per capita income began to catch up with the Western world, first in Japan and then in China, that their respective governments and a growing international clientele began to see Japanese and Chinese[25] as valuable in the marketplace of languages and hence worth acquiring.

Language dissemination policies could long be seen as a manifestation of a European- and then Western-centric world carrying with it its colonial legacy. The fact that the two modernization latecomers mentioned above then claimed a place on the international stage of language promotion was not always welcome, especially in the case of China, which does not necessarily accept the ideas and norms set by Western powers. This can be seen as a manifestation of the 'clash of civilizations' diagnosed by American political scientist Samuel P. Huntington on the threshold of the twenty-first century. Confucius Institutes were initially welcomed throughout the Western world because, to put it bluntly, they brought money for financing language education. In recent years, however, Confucius Institutes, most of which operate on university campuses, have met with much criticism and quite a few have been closed down because of their relationship to the Chinese Communist Party, the policies and propaganda of the Chinese government, or because of their actual or assumed role in knowledge transfer and infringement of intellectual property rights (Yuan, Guo and Zhu 2016). If proof was needed of the potentially contentious nature of language dissemination policy, China's strategy for spreading the Chinese language around the world is a case in point.

The difference between the reception of Japanese and Chinese language dissemination agencies is conspicuous. Japan aligned herself with the West after World War II; China did not. Japan Foundation activities rarely make headlines in Western countries. Confucius Institutes do, often being portrayed, rightly or wrongly, as expressions of Chinese imperialism, especially where the influence of Western imperialism was strongest, in Africa. By 2022, there were 61 Confucius Institutes in 46 African countries, all of which China has diplomatic relations with. China's language dissemination policy is intertwined with the political and economic agenda of strengthening China's influence on the continent. While this must be disturbing from the perspective that sees the division of Africa into anglophone, francophon,e and lusophone countries as the natural order of things, it only reminds us of the intimate connection between language and power and that, accordingly, the linguistic map of the world is always just a snapshot. While Makoni's question whether 'Chinese will be Africa's next lingua franca' (Makoni et al. 2012: 541) may have been a bit audacious, it seems that on the continent that has the most experience with imperial language policies Chinese fell on fertile ground. In some countries, South Africa leading the way, it is now integrated in the foreign language education system. Should this be considered an encroachment into the institutions of African countries? This is an intriguing question to be carefully examined in the context of comparative politics, but which goes beyond the scope of this book (see, e.g., Li 2021). What is clear, however, is that China's international language promotion policy is an intervention into the area of soft power that for some time seemed to be the prerogative of Western powers.[26]

From a scholarly point of view, China's Confucius Institutes bring the power dimension of cultural policies into focus. The worldwide spread of European languages was originally part of the civilizing mission, which arguably contributed more than anything else to the international politicization of language.

Policies must constantly change as power relations, socio-economic transformations, and technical innovations require adjustments. At present, we are living through a period of such change triggered by China's rise on one hand, and the digital turn on the other. What this means for language academies and language dissemination agencies we are only beginning to understand. New challenges for language policy include the question of the norm-setting authority—government departments, state-sponsored academies, or profit-seeking companies—as well as the dissemination of languages in the internet by state agents or independent thereof. To what extent the supranational conventions that are taking shape in certain environments will be supported by national legislations remains to be seen, a question to be discussed in the next chapter.

Further reading

Radtke, Edgar, Sybille Große, Ekkehard Felder, Ronja Grebe. 2019. Language institutions and language criticism in European perspective. *Handbuch Europäische Sprachkritik Online*, vol. 4, Sprachinstitutionen und Sprachkritik. https://doi.org/10.17885/heiup.heso.2019.1.24071

Stickel, Gerhard (ed.) 2018. *National language institutions and national languages. Contributions to the EFNIL Conference 2017 in Mannheim*. Budapest: Research Institute for Linguistics, Hungarian Academy of Sciences. Accessible through the EFNIL website at: http://www.efnil.org

Thomas, George. 1991. *Linguistic Purism*. London: Longman.

Zhou, Minglang and Hongkai Sun (eds.) 2004. *Language Policy in the People's Republic of China. Theory and Practice Since 1949*. Boston: Kluwer Academic Publishers.

7

International language regimes

> New York: Prime Minister Narendra Modi spoke in Hindi as he addressed the UN General Assembly session in New York on Saturday, emulating his party, the BJP's iconic leader and former prime minister Atal Behari Vajpayee.
>
> Since taking charge as Prime Minister in May, Mr Modi has stuck to Hindi for most of his speeches and interactions with world leaders. Only after the historic entry of India's Mangalyaan into the Mars orbit earlier this week, did he use more than a smattering of English while addressing space scientists. NDTV 27 September 2014[1]
>
> India donates $1 mn to promote Hindi at UN. The Meghalayan 19 July 2023

Considered as a whole, the international language regime in the sense of regulating communications between states, organizations, and individuals is part of and reflects a Eurocentric world. A hundred years ago, this was even more pronounced, giving us a point of departure for discussing this area of language policy.

Hope

Communicating across borders, political and linguistic ones, has always been difficult, with the power differences between the countries involved not being the least of the problems. When the guns were silenced and

Language Policy. Florian Coulmas, Oxford University Press. © Florian Coulmas (2025).
DOI: 10.1093/9780191976377.003.0007

the world was trying to come to terms with the devastation of the First World War at the Paris Peace Conference there was general agreement that it was more important than ever to talk with each other. To this end the Société des Nations/League of Nations was established as the world's first intergovernmental organization. The 42 founding members believed that rather than on the battlefield solutions to disputes should be sought at the negotiation table. *How* their delegates should speak to each other was less of an issue than *that* they did it.

That the official languages of the League would be French and English, the languages of then still the largest empires, was a matter of course, although there was some discontent, because participants who did not speak these languages well were at a disadvantage. Early on, the Japanese delegate Nitobe Inazō, himself a fluent speaker of English who, in his capacity as delegate of the League, had just visited the thirteenth International Esperanto Congress, 1921, in Prague, therefore submitted a proposal to the League to adopt Esperanto as working language. His arguments to the effect that a language which no one owned and which was not designed to replace other languages would allow all delegates to meet on an equal footing and thus help the League to become a fair and egalitarian organization were convincing. Ten of 11 members of the Council of the League supported the motion. Only Gabriel Hanotaux, the French delegate and a member of the Académie française, voted against it and used France's veto power in the council to bring down the project.

Power reflected

The hope embodied by Esperanto, which literally means 'the one who hopes', came to nothing, but the topic of languages in intergovernmental organizations was put on the agenda. The League's successor organization, the United Nations, founded by 51 states after the Second World War in 1945, established by its General Assembly in 1946 Chinese, English, French, Russian, and Spanish as official languages and French and English as working languages. In subsequent years, the UN's language regime was amended repeatedly, making Spanish a working language in 1948 and the same for Russian in 1969 and Chinese in 1973. Also in 1973, Arabic was included as official language and working language of the General Assembly, and Chinese was added as a working language of the Security Council. In 1982, Arabic was added to the official and working languages of the Security Council.[2]

Compared to the two official languages of the League of Nations, the six official languages of the United Nations represent a move away from outright Western (linguistic) dominance towards a more balanced language regime. Two non-European languages were now part of the UN language regime, which would have been very unlikely at the time of the League when decolonization was still in its infancy. The geopolitics of language is clearly visible here. Historically contingent as it is, the UN language regime has what those concerned consider deficiencies. Given that in 2023 the number of UN members was almost four times what it was in the year of its foundation, 193 plus two observer states, this is not surprising and raises several obvious questions regarding the hierarchization of languages. Why does Hindi not enjoy official status, the third most populous language on earth ahead of both Spanish and French? Why not Portuguese, Indonesian, Turkish, Japanese, or German? The answers to these questions are well known. For example, defeated in World War II, Japan and Germany were not involved in the creation of the UN and called 'enemy states' in the UN Charter. At the time Hindi was still a language of a British colony, and Indonesia, too, did not exist as a sovereign nation. As soon as the language regime of the UN was established, it thus came under pressure to adapt and still is, as power relations change. To dwell on the example just mentioned, post-World War II reconstruction restored both Japan and Germany to become powerful countries, which for some time now have been the third and fourth largest contributors, respectively, to the UN budget, after the US and China. Yet, their voice remains unheard, at least on the symbolic level of official languages.

Changes in language regimes, even if desired, are not implemented easily, first of all because the beneficiaries of the extant regime will defend it, and because language policy always has functional and symbolic aspects. Granting official status to a language is a matter of prestige which, however, makes little sense unless it can be assured that the language in question can be used for the tasks associated with that status. Using a language in international contexts for diplomacy, dealing with world affairs, and translating official documents is demanding, since such documents include, among others, meeting records and summaries, announcements of new initiatives, resolutions from legislative bodies, declarations of intent, contracts and treaties containing very specialized technical terminology.

Acknowledging and thereby supporting humanity's linguistic multitude, the UN proudly advertises the Universal Declaration of Human Rights in 549 (2023) different languages,[3] but this is just the beginning of a long path towards the development of compatible legal terminologies in many languages. It is not for nothing that the working languages of the International Court of Justice, the principal judicial organ of the United Nations, are only two, English and French. Streamlining procedures and keeping translation and interpreting costs down play a role here, but the intricacies of legal terminology is a factor as well. Conceptual problems in translating legal texts are rife even among European languages and occupy a central position in comparative law. Crossing the borders to languages that evolved in the context of other legal traditions is even more challenging and makes adapting language regimes with legal implications difficult. The very concept of case law is testimony to the sociohistorical embeddedness of law and the languages used to give it expression.

The secretariat of the UN is keenly aware of the skewed nature of the UN language regime, but increasing the number of official languages at the various levels of the UN system can only make the work of the UN more cumbersome; and once a serious initiative would be taken to this end, the question of which languages should be given official status is likely to be controversial. Conversely, reducing the number of official languages would be equally controversial and met with opposition. Therefore, for the time being, the UN has to live with its current language regime, which is unlikely to be changed in the near future, although everyone knows its shortcomings.

In addition to the imperfect representation of the world's languages, the UN language regime faces another problem. Its six official languages are nominally equal, but far from it in practice. To acknowledge this inequity and correct it, its Department of Global Communications has established 'language days' for each of the UN's six official languages. The purpose of this programme is 'to eliminate the disparity between the use of English and the use of the other five official languages' and, in the spirit of the times, 'to celebrate multilingualism and cultural diversity as well as to promote equal use of all six official languages throughout the Organization'.[4] The initiative to enhance the UN web multilingualism exemplifies the gap between policy goals and implementation, between symbolic commitments and actual behaviour. The difference between official language and working language is indicative of the same tension which can be observed in several UN agencies and programmes. The six official languages have equal status, but some are more equal than others, if only because the role these languages play outside the UN system cannot but also affect their use within it. When it comes to serious business, symbolic frills are expendable, and we all know what serious 'business' is in the neoliberal world. The International Monetary Fund hence uses only English. The World Trade Organization admits French and Spanish in addition to English, as indicated in Table 7 which offers an overview of the language regimes of major intergovernmental organizations. If limiting the use of English is one of its language policy objectives, the UN is fighting an uphill battle. Theoretically this is interesting because, as pointed out in the previous chapter (Chapter 6), unlike other former colonial languages English spread as the language of power without much centralized administrative regulation and support. It is widely used as a colonial legacy and a matter of convenience rather than taste.

This legacy has been the subject of intense discussions and contrary positions among scholars active in the field of language policy. The notion of 'linguistic imperialism' mentioned in Chapter 6 is one view on the role of English in the world today. By its advocates it is associated with the neoliberal economic order, especially its negative sides that enhance homogenization, drive competitors out of business, and pose a threat to the small and the weak. They consider the promotion of 'linguistic human rights'[5] as the only promising alternative for creating a 'better world' where equality is guaranteed and all speakers enjoy the same right to use their language. An opposite view has long been held by

Belgian political philosopher Philippe Van Parijs (2011) who highlights the benefits of a global lingua franca, especially for low-income countries where poor people are more interested in enhancing their skills for the labour market than in equal treatment of languages. The inherent injustice of the privileged status of the English language cannot be denied. Some want to correct it, others accept it as a historical fact. But where are the policies, if any, that could change it and bring about more justice and equality? While this remains an open question, the debate between these two positions has shed some light on an important LP dimension to which we will return in the next chapter, economic interests.[6] The fact that English enjoys official status in more countries than any other language (Table 6), not only has obvious implications for its position in the language regimes of international organizations, but also makes it economically most valuable.

Table 6 The ten top languages by number of countries in which they have official status

Language	Number of countries
English	59
French	29
Arabic	23
Spanish	20
Portuguese	9
German	6
Russian	5
Swahili	5
Italian	4
Malay	4

It should be noted that both columns of Table 6 look more definitive than they are. The number 23 for Arabic, for example, includes Palestine, where Arabic is spoken, the political status of which is, however, disputed. Similarly, Macau, is counted among the Portuguese speaking polities, although it is a Special Administrative Region of China, where moreover it is hardly spoken any more. On the other side, for Malay four countries are counted, Malaysia, Indonesia, Brunei, and Singapore, although, as we have seen above (p. 91), Indonesia has strenuously worked for linguistic separatism. When we look at the bigger picture, polities and languages are less stable than numbers suggest; nevertheless, Table 6 suffices to illustrate the power relations between languages in the contemporary world and shows us one reason why the disparity between the use of English and the other five official UN languages is hard to eliminate. Table 7 reveals additional reasons for this.

The language regimes of intergovernmental organizations usually reveal something about their history. For example, the Universal Postal Union (UPU), a specialized agency of the UN, but founded in the nineteenth century in Bern, Switzerland, used to have French as its sole official language. Once it became evident that many more postal clerks around the world were proficient in English than in French, English was in 1994 added as a working language. The UPU makes most of its documents available in the UN official languages and Portuguese. Official and working language status is important because it is indicative of inequality and the status of languages and the standing of their respective countries in the world. It does not, however, restrict the activities of these organizations in other languages, which is more important in some organizations than in others. For instance, various activities of the World Health Organization, another subsidiary of the UN, often target population groups who may not know any of the official UN languages, but for which a broad understanding is critical to success. In order to deal with the outbreak of Covid-19 it set up a programme to inform and train health professionals, decision makers, and the general public in 70 languages.[7] Needless to say, these were national languages only, because the WHO depends on national governments' cooperation and because the programme is about training and disseminating information rather than language policy in support of minority languages.

UNICEF is another case in point. Operating in any of the official UN languages, mostly English and French, the United Nations Children's Fund pays much attention to the influence of language policy on school education, especially at the elementary level. In multilingual post-colonial countries, colonial/international languages are often seen as gateway to 'global citizenship' and therefore prioritized by education policy makers, while studies have repeatedly shown that a language

Table 7 Official (o) and working (w) languages of major international organizations

Language IGO	Arabic A	Chinese C	English E	French F	Russian R	Spanish S	Interpre-tation
Common-wealth of Nations			o				
ICC	o	o	o, w	o, w	o	o	
ILO			o	o		o	
IMF			o				A, C, F, R, S, Japanese
IOC			o	o			A, R, S, German
IPU			o	o			A, S
ITU			o	o		o	
OECD			o	o			
UN	o	o	o	o	o	o	
UNEP	o	o	o	o	o	o	
UPU			w	o			
WB			o				A, C, F, R, S
WHO	o	o	o	o	o	o	
WTO			o	o		o	

Abbreviations: IGO Intergovernmental Organisation, ICC International Criminal Court, ILO International Labour Organisation, IMF International Monetary Fund, IOC International Olympic Committee, IPU Inter-Parliamentary Union, ITU International Telecommunication Union, OECD Organisation for Co-operation and Development, UN United Nations, UNEP United Nations Environmental Programme, UPU Universal Postal Union, WB World Bank, WHO World Health Organisation, WTO World Trade Organisation that is well understood by the target audience, that is, pupils and their parents, have a better effect on learning. UNICEF therefore promotes awareness-raising campaigns regarding pedagogic and political implications of language choice at school in the interest of improving learning outcomes.[8]

The UN is committed to multilingualism and has adopted and implemented policies to that end, being convinced that it 'facilitates the cause of the United Nations with respect to maintaining peace and security, promoting human rights and the rule of law, and conducting operational activities for sustainable development'.[9] High expectations, no doubt, but not shared by all intergovernmental organizations.

Symbolism, pragmatism

Linguistic multitude is in any case a factor affecting international language regimes, implying direct and indirect costs in budgetary terms and operational efficiency. The United Nations' language services account for only a relatively small share of its annual budget, where 'relatively' means as a percentage of the total budget. The cost of other organizations' language services may be lower or higher, but there are costs, and they can affect the types of services set up by these organizations. The organizations listed in Table 7 make use between one and four official and working languages. The Association of Southeast Asian Nations, ASEAN, which promotes intergovernmental cooperation focussing mainly on economic integration, comprises an estimated population of some 670 million. It makes do with just one working language. The choice of English, a foreign language for all members, suggests that this is not or not only because of budgetary considerations. Rather, the great linguistic diversity of the ten member states, which have some 130 languages on average each, would make it very difficult to select and agree on a manageable number of official languages. Spoken in four member states as an official language, Malay would be the strongest candidate to serve as ASEAN's official or working language; however, it is not widely used in the other countries and differs greatly from their national languages.

In the African Union the colonial languages English, French, Portuguese, and Spanish, all of which are official in some African states (see Chapter 5), are official and, as stated in the Protocol on the Amendments to the Constitutive Act of the AU of 2003, 'Kiswahili and any other African language'. Such blanket recognition of African languages suggests that official status has mainly symbolic meaning and does not necessarily affect actual language choice in official contexts. The tension between the felt need to give African languages a proper place in an African institution and their politically subordinate position in most African states is tangible here. The language regime of the East African Community (EAC) exhibits a similar tendency, although the status of Kiswahili, which rose to national language in Tanzania, Kenya, Uganda, and the Democratic Republic of the Congo, is more specific there than that of 'any African language' in the AU. Arabic and Kiswahili are the only African languages used by the intergovernmental organizations listed in Table 7. The only other non-European language we find in the table is Guarani, a South American language spoken by a community of some 6.5 million in Paraguay, Bolivia, Argentina, and Brazil. Still, functioning in Portuguese and Spanish, Mercosur, like COMESA, are yet two other organizations that embody the dominance of European languages the age of colonialism has left behind. Only in recent decades have other languages entered the scene, Russian in CIS formed after the disintegration of the Soviet Union, and Russian and Chinese in the SCO, a potentially powerful organization founded in 2001 that has yet to demonstrate its influence on the global scene.

The most expensive language regime: 'resource-efficient full multilingualism'

'Multilingualism remains essential to multilateral communications', says the UN.[10] 'The co-existence of many languages in Europe is a powerful symbol of the European Union's (EU) aspiration to be united in diversity', says the European Commission.[11] No other intergovernmental organization accepts and applies the principle spelt out by the UN more persistently than the EU; at a cost. A political entity that actually operates in 24 languages and does not only use them for symbolic purposes has no rival. The EU's official languages are Bulgarian, Croatian, Czech, Danish, Dutch, English, Estonian, Finnish, French, German, Greek, Hungarian, Irish, Italian, Latvian, Lithuanian, Maltese, Polish, Portuguese, Romanian, Slovak, Slovenian, Spanish, and Swedish. What next? At the time of writing these lines, Albania, Moldova, North Macedonia, Montenegro, Serbia, Turkey, and Ukraine had applied for EU membership and been declared candidate countries by the European Commission between 1999, Turkey, and 2022, Ukraine. The current 24 official languages make for a total of 552 combinations for translation and interpretations. If all seven candidates were admitted, and of their languages we would group Montenegrin, North Macedonian, and Serbian as related varieties together with Croatian, and Moldovan with Romanian, still three new languages, Albanian, Turkish, and Ukrainian, would have to be integrated in the system, resulting in 702 combinations for translation and interpretation. And so on. The timeline that led from four official EU languages in 1958 to 24 in 2013 would then be extrapolated accordingly (Table 8).

Table 8 Timeline of expansion of the number of official languages of the EU

1958:	Dutch, French, German, Italian*
1973:	Danish, English
1981:	Greek
1986:	Portuguese, Spanish
1995:	Finnish, Swedish
2004:	Czech, Estonian, Hungarian, Latvian, Lithuanian, Maltese, Polish, Slovak, Slovene
2007:	Bulgarian, Irish, Romanian
2013:	Croatian

*At the time, the European Economic Community

'United in diversity' sounds like a catchy advertising slogan, rather than an admission that the national languages ideology that spread in Europe since the French Revolution and has been strengthened by universal education, the media, and nationalist policies is as deep-rooted as ever and has always stood in the way of developing an EU language policy in its own right. This is reflected in what the EU does not do: it does not agree on a single working language, and it does not recognize languages other than the members' national languages, where 'national' refers to a nation state rather than a nationality, such as Catalan (see p. 74). If evidence was necessary that a pluralist international society is impossible to achieve, the EU is the paradigm example. To put it less negatively, the EU is an international society of a special kind united by common interests and divided by linguistic multitude.

If the 'co-existence of many (national) languages in Europe is a powerful symbol', it is also a considerable challenge for policy makers and administrators. Against this background, the EU has created the most expensive and, measured by its tasks, most efficient language service of any international organization. The European Parliament's translation service alone has a staff of some 1150, and there are others. In addition to the European Parliament, the Translation Centre for the Bodies of the European Union[12] serves the Council of the European Union, the European Commission, the Court of Justice of the EU, the European Central Bank, the European Investment Bank, the European Court of Auditors, and the consultative bodies the European Economic and Social Committee and the European Committee of the Regions. Interpreting and translating for these EU bodies is so important in the EU's self-understanding because it is a matter of democratic control, transparency, and hence legitimacy. The ambitious goal is to enable all citizens of the Union to communicate with EU institutions and to access laws and other documents issued by the European Parliament and other institutions in their own languages (where 'their own languages', of course, only covers the 24 official languages of the EU). This policy goal is enshrined in the EU's Charter of Fundamental Rights and the Treaty on the Functioning of the European Union.

This treaty emphasizes the 'objective of respecting the Union's rich cultural and linguistic diversity' and includes 'the right to petition the European Parliament, to apply to the European Ombudsman, and to address the institutions and advisory bodies of the Union in any of the Treaty languages and to obtain a reply in the same language' (Article 20). How language is taken seriously in the context of EU institutions and how thoroughly it is regulated emerges from declarations concerning the provisions of the EU treaties such as this one by the Republic of Latvia, the Republic of Hungary, and the Republic of Malta on the spelling of the name of the single currency in the treaties:

> Without prejudice to the unified spelling of the name of the single currency of the European Union referred to in the Treaties as displayed on the banknotes and on the coins, Latvia, Hungary and Malta declare that the spelling of the name of the single currency, including its derivatives as applied throughout the Latvian, Hungarian and Maltese text of the Treaties, has no effect on the existing rules of the Latvian, Hungarian or Maltese languages.[13]

Spelling, if you ever had any doubts about it, is not a petty trifle, but can be a matter of national significance, at least in certain contexts, as in this example of the spelling of the currency's name—the Euro being spelt *eurót* in Hungarian, *eiro* in Latvian, and *Ewro* in Maltese—and wherever human behaviour is regulated by law. This declaration also serves as a reminder that both language and money are means of exchange that fulfil many similar functions (see Chapter 8).

Law is language, and since the EU is committed to the rule of law it must pay due attention to language, not any language, that is, but the language(s) in which the law is drawn up. When we search the website of the European Commission for the phrase 'official languages' we are offered 664,222 search results, in English. Multiply this by 24 and you get yet another confirmation of the central role attributed to national languages in the EU. Most important, Regulation No 1 from 1958, as amended, of the Treaty on the Functioning of the European Union stipulates that EU institutions have 24 official and working languages.[14] Just proclaiming this kind of institutional multilingualism is not enough; it must be organized. To this end, and because it is quite costly, the EU Parliament has adopted a Code of Conduct on Multilingualism that on some 18 pages regulates the use of language services. Among many other provisions it stipulates that 'members' language-related rights shall be governed by Parliament's Rules of Procedure [...] and be guaranteed on the basis of the principles governing "resource-efficient full multilingualism"'.[15] Flagrant waste is obvious, for example, mistakenly calling interpreters of a language to a meeting where no one speaks it, but in many other cases resource-efficiency is difficult to measure. The rules of procedure of the European Parliament are therefore very detailed. Rule 167, for example, provides that (1) all documents shall be drawn up in the official languages, and (3) interpretation shall be provided in committee and delegation meetings from and into the official languages that are used and requested by the members.[16] The intricacies of translation and law were mentioned above (p. 110). In order to assure conformity of law across all member states, Article 5 of the same rule states that 'after the result of a vote has been announced, the President shall rule on any requests concerning alleged discrepancies between the different language versions'. The presence of such an article indicates that language-related differences in legislation and jurisdiction have to be reckoned with and must be corrected to secure uniformity of law throughout the EU.

Given the volume of translations in the European Parliament, in the other EU bodies, and the legal significance of many of these documents, language-related differences are certain to occur. Since 1994 when the Translation Centre of the EU was founded until 2020, it translated some 13.4 million pages into and from the official languages.[17] Linguistic verification and legal-linguistic finalization of legally relevant documents are required, as detailed in Article 9 of the Code of Conduct on Multilingualism of the European Parliament.

In sum, by using its official languages for purposes of legislation and jurisdiction, the EU has in effect strongly reinforced the national language system that evolved in Europe as an integral part of the nation state system. At the same time, the EU language regime has had an unanticipated and, for some members, unwelcome consequence in further strengthening the position of English. As early as the turn of the century, the influential sociologist of language Abram De Swaan (2001) pointed out that more languages within the EU could only mean more English. Since the time of his writing when French was still widely spoken by the EU, bureaucracy, and in the corridors of power, this prediction has certainly been born out. The number of official EU languages doubled and French has been sidelined in many domains, since English has become the uncontested first foreign language in all member states, old and new.

It is preferentially used in all informal and formal meetings held without interpreters as a matter of convenience as much as the principle of 'resource-efficient full multilingualism' (cf. also Gazzola 2016).

The irony of this development is that the UK never embraced the EU wholeheartedly. If on the threshold of the twenty-first century, Brexit was not quite on the horizon, few were really surprised when, after protracted negotiations following the EU membership referendum of 2016, in 2022 it happened. The only lasting legacy of the UK's 49 year-membership seems to be the English language, which continues to be predominant in EU institutions. The fact that English is co-official with Irish and Maltese in Ireland and Malta, respectively, does not make English an EU language on a par with French, Italian, German, etc. It has been a long-standing EU policy to recognize one language per member state. Maltese became an EU language when Malta joined the bloc in 2004, and Irish was granted official status in 2022[18] for which Ireland had lobbied since 1973. In the EU, English therefore no longer has an actual home country that justifies its official status in the EU. But it is indispensable.

With regard to its language policy, the prominence of English in the EU raises several questions. The most general one is whether the EU actually has a language policy or whether what it calls one is really a capitulation to market forces. We have seen above that multilingualism in the EU is subject to considerable symbolic and financial backing, which would support the argument that the Union does have a consciously designed and agreed-upon language policy. As I have tried to show, this policy is grounded in the ideology of the national language, which in turn is closely associated with the nation state, a structure that unlike the empires it replaced thrives on inclusion and exclusion. And that's why this policy is outdated, because the nation state system is.

At the present time, resurgent nationalism is often observed, recent political spasms in the US, Italy, France, and Germany serving as examples, not to mention Eastern European countries led by Hungary and Poland. Nevertheless, despite its outdated language policy, the EU is an experiment to transcend the nation state system which, one should not forget, has not been the universal template of political organization for much more than a century. In Europe it worked quite well, if we forget about the Second World War and take the development of Western welfare states as a measure. But if we look beyond the confines of the West to post-colonial areas, it is obvious that national self-determination modelled on the European pattern has been unable to deliver on the promises of law and order, freedom, security, and welfare.

Today, the nation state system is undermined from within and without. In terms of language policy, the call for 'diversity' in defence of minority languages has grown louder over the past two or three decades, while national solipsism has become increasingly difficult to sustain against the forces of transnationalism and globalization. While politics still mostly remain in national disputes, the drivers of global change are economic and technological forces that neoliberal capitalism has largely freed from national control. Brexit well illustrates these dynamics. Dreams of past imperial grandeur and resentment against the 'bureaucratic monster' of Brussels may be held by many, but will not bring back the place Great Britain once had in the world. What sustains Britain's global reach today is more than anything else the English language, which spread around the globe promoted by above all economic forces. This is one reason why we have to take a closer look at the economic dimensions of language policy, which we will do in the next chapter.

Further reading

De Swaan, Abram. 2001. *Words of the World. The Global Language System.* Cambridge: Polity Press.

Language Policy. Fact Sheets on the European Union. European Parliament. https://www.europarl.europa.eu/factsheets/en/sheet/142/language-policy

Lozinskiy, Nikolay. 2020. *Multilingualism in the United Nations System.* Geneva: United Nations. https://www.unjiu.org/sites/www.unjiu.org/files/jiu_rep_2020_6_english.pdf

Mignolo, Walter. 2001. Géopolitique de la connaissance, colonialité de pouvoir e difference colonial. *Multitudes*, September, 56–71.

8

Language policy and the wealth of nations

> It is precisely because language consumers see language as an economic good that individuals and communities tend to acquire high-yield languages. They gravitate towards languages that accrue more economic returns for their investment of time and intellectual efforts. Under normal circumstances, language consumers will invest their talents in learning a language that is economically or politically profitable for them (Koffi 2012: 253).

Can language policy withstand economic interest? This is the overarching question discussed in this chapter. In order to discuss it, we have to first of all fathom the economic dimensions of language which emerge, for example, from titles of journal articles such as these: 'Language and trade; language and foreign direct investment; linguistic diversity and poverty; the role of language policy in poverty alleviation; occupational foreign language use; wage gaps between speakers of different languages; bilingualism and earnings; linguistic distance and applied economics; language as human capital; language and development.' Published in economics and sociological journals, these articles among many others demonstrate some of the reasons why economic aspects of language and linguistic aspects of the economy, as motivating factors and conditions of successful implementation, are of considerable importance to language policy.

Language Policy. Florian Coulmas, Oxford University Press. © Florian Coulmas (2025).
DOI: 10.1093/9780191976377.003.0008

Means of exchange

There are 195 sovereign states in the world today, 2025. In these countries, 180 currencies are recognized as legal tender, a small numerical difference which, however, if we assume that there is no country without a monetary means of exchange, is indicative of the fact that some currencies are used in more than one country. This is evidently so, if we just think of the EU. It introduced the euro as an accounting currency in 1999, which then entered actual circulation in 2002, and is today used as the official currency in 19 EU member states. Giving up the French franc, the deutschmark, the Italian lira, the Dutch guilder etc. was a political decision of major consequence justified by the expectation that it would maximize economic efficiency. This expectation was born out, at least in the affluent northern EU member states, though less so in southern European countries, especially Greece, which was most severely affected by economic hardship, sky-high unemployment rates, and a government debt of 180 per cent of GDP in the wake of the 2008 financial crisis. The monetary union deprived Greece of the possibility of devaluing the drachma—its currency from 1833 to 2001—by buying up its own government bonds through its central bank. As a result, Greece would have collapsed under the load of its debt without bailout loans by the European Central Bank and the International Monetary Fund.

There are strong and weak currencies, important and unimportant currencies, currencies that are held in reserve by the International Monetary Fund (IMF)—currently only five, US dollar, euro, Chinese yuan, Japanese yen, and British pound—and the rest of them that are not; convertible and non-convertible currencies; currencies that are pegged to others, and currencies that stand alone. The ideal territorial extent of a currency has long been the subject of economic studies, and Moscow's insistence during Russia's war on Ukraine that LNG deliveries should only be paid for in roubles is a telling example of the political-economic importance of currencies. In international trade, those whose currencies are used have an advantage. It was for this reason that, at the Bretton Woods Conference of 1944, which was intended to regulate the international financial and monetary order after World War II, the

British government proposed introducing the *bancor* as an international currency for world trade. The bancor was the brainchild of famous economist and one of the architects of the IMF John Maynard Keynes who, with some ideas of fairness in mind, saw the need for a universal auxiliary currency.[1] It was not adopted at the conference, and somewhat later US economist Charles Kindleberger argued against an international means of exchange because, he contended, the US dollar fulfilled this role.[2]

If Kindleberger's rejection of the bancor reminds you of Gabriel Hanotaux's veto mentioned above (Chapter 7) against Esperanto as the working language of the League of Nations because French fulfilled this role, you will certainly also recognize the analogy of currency and language as means of exchange in international relations, where both are subject to power competition. Currency exchange contributes to transaction cost for those who do not use the US dollar domestically, as does translation for those who do not use the language of international trade domestically. The parallel goes further than that. Indian economist Krishna S. Dhir observes that just like currencies are used to account for value, store value, and exchange value, languages are used to account for knowledge and information, store knowledge and information, and exchange knowledge and information.[3] There is an international monetary system and there is an international language system, and both are about conventions without substance. My money has value only because people trust that it is valuable, just as my words have meaning only because other people think they have. That /yama/ means 'mountain' in Japanese and 'hole' in Russian, that English /beter/ means 'worse' in Turkish, and /gift/ means 'present' in English and 'poison' in German are just three of infinitely many examples of the conventional nature of words. They are like little pieces of paper with some cypher printed on them without inherent value/meaning. Trust is decisive—so help us god, as Americans are reminded on every dollar bill. Others put a portrait of the president, queen, or other person of honour on their banknotes to lend them a degree of trustworthiness. These are political decisions, for monetary phenomena, like linguistic phenomena, are political. As means of trusting exchange, languages and currencies are commons of communities, large or small, that benefit rather than are depleted from being used by their members, who as individuals are not able to determine the purchasing power of their coins or the meaning of their words. Just as there is no private currency, there is no private language.

Currencies and languages are both instruments and symbols of power. On the international plane, US hegemony is reflected and recognized around the globe by people paying with dollars and using English as the number one world language, while few things manifest China's recent ascent more clearly than the inclusion of the yuan, which until then most people considered a basket case, in the IMF's reserve currencies basket in 2016.[4] Whether Chinese will become a language of wider communication is an open question to which we will briefly turn below. If so, it will take time, as it did for English, French, Spanish, and Portuguese, to be imposed on/acquired by speakers of other languages in the colonial age. In any case, even though money has no intrinsic value and language no intrinsic meaning, these two means of exchange make the world go round. The last half century has seen the deregulation of monetary exchange and financial markets that have never been ideologized to the extent that languages have in nineteenth-century Europe, which is one reason why states still cling to their national languages. The fact that the EU was able to agree on a common currency, but not on a common language, not even as a bureaucratic working language, is a vivid expression of this difference between currencies and languages, which otherwise have so many functions in common.

Language as human capital

Languages can be and are acquired and can therefore be conceived of as a kind of wealth or 'linguistic capital', as sociologist Pierre Bourdieu argued. Since in the neoliberal world everything is commercialized, so is language (Heller 2018). Teachers, interpreters, translators, publishers, diplomats, journalists, and international marketing experts, among others, can earn a living with their language skills, and some of them now fear being displaced by artificial intelligence programmes.[5] Migrant workers need at least elementary language skills to find a job. Bourdieu noted about linguistic capital and its distribution 'the simple fact that a competence has value only so long as it has a market'.[6] What this 'simple fact' immediately reveals is the fundamental inequality of the world's languages with respect to the social, political, and economic functions they perform. A few of them—the 'high-yield languages' of the beginning of the chapter—are traded, marketed, and acquired for gain, while for the vast majority of all languages no market exists. Attempts have been made to counter the imbalance between marketable and not marketable languages, for instance, the EU Commission's multilingualism policy (see below). There is also considerable support for minority languages by their speakers as well as civil society organizations, but in societies permeated by neoliberalism it is an uphill battle.

The strength of high-yield languages in the EU can be observed throughout the world. Leading the field of languages of wider communication, English can be put to use in many places and in many professions, which is a strong incentive for learning it. Annually more than 550,000 international students come to the UK to study English. The value of the English language teaching (ELT) industry that evolved to satisfy this demand is estimated to be worth £1.4 billion a year.[7] The economic benefits of English for the UK are enormous;[8] however, they would not be generated if the customers of the ELT industry did not in turn expect economic benefits from their efforts. Adam Smith[9] trumps William Shakespeare. Acquiring English is an investment which can be compared with the acquisition of other languages by individuals and public and private collective actors. Learning a language requires time and effort, but an investment in learning one language, say, Mapuche, a language spoken in Chile, is likely to yield a lesser economic return than learning another, Spanish, also spoken in Chile.

This is where language policy, acquisition policy in particular, comes into play. National and regional governments make decisions about school curricula including foreign language education, decisions that are influenced by tradition, culture, but also, and increasingly nowadays, by economic considerations relating to individuals, a country, or, as in the case of the EU just mentioned, a multinational organization. After the disintegration of the Soviet Union, foreign language curricula in most Eastern European countries saw a switch from Russian as first foreign language to English or German, the language of the economic powerhouse nearby. Some Eastern European governments went further than that and initiated national language policies that, if not in name, were anti-Russian in substance. A case in point is the adoption of 'The Amendment Law to the Basic School and Gymnasium Law and Other Laws (Transition to Estonian-Language Education) 722 SE' by the Estonian Parliament in December 2022, which establishes that the full transition to Estonian-language education will start in 2024 and would be finalized by 2030.[10] Latvia passed a similar law designed to make Latvian the sole language of instruction in schools, which met with harsh criticism by the UN (Camut 2023). The fact that the proportion of L1 Russian speakers in both countries is over 20 per cent of the population makes this criticism understandable and is at the same time a vivid example of the fact that language policy decisions are hard to appreciate without considering their historical background.

In the case of the shift from Russian to English or German as first foreign language taught at school, government policies coincided with public demand; but this is not always the case. In multilingual India, to return to the example mentioned at the beginning of Chapter 2, the government has for some time promoted Hindi in order to maintain or create a sense of national community and to curb the use of the 'colonial language'; but as urban Indians all know, employment opportunities requiring English skills—not just in call-centres—are plentiful, which keeps a strong demand for English alive, also and especially as language of instruction at school. Government policies and economic preferences are hence hard to make compatible. Torn between national pride and economic utility, language policies in the educational sector are often contested in India, as mentioned in Chapter 6.

This kind of tension between policies which aim to regulate social behaviour and economically motivated language choices have been observed in many countries. At the turn of the century, Canadian geolinguist Roland J.L. Breton asked: 'Can English be dethroned?' His considerations showed this to be a largely rhetorical question because, he argued, economic globalization favours English and the world domination of English 'is deliberately organised by the Anglo-Saxon powers'.[11] English is, of course, not the only language that embodies linguistic capital and is traded on the language market, but at this time it is the economically most valuable one globally.

Language ranking

If, for the time being, because of the economic incentive to learn it, English cannot be dethroned, its utility can be compared to that of other languages. This is politically relevant as utility measures, cost-benefit analysis, and rankings have permeated virtually every area of political decision making. Various schemes of assessing the utility of a language, its communication potential, its economic value, or however you want to call it, have been proposed in recent decades.[12] To this end, meaningful criteria are needed.

Perhaps the most obvious measure of the importance of a language is the size of its speech community. Language serves the function of connecting its users, and the more speakers it has, the more opportunities it offers each one of them. Every additional speaker adds to the value of the language in question, for themselves and all others, which results in a circular, self-reinforcing process.

Though an important parameter, the size of the L1 speech community is not a robust criterion of a language's economic value. Both Mandarin Chinese and Hindi have more L1 speakers than English, but their utility on the global scale is certainly less. This is so because these two languages are much more geographically concentrated than English and English has more L2 speakers than they do. Geographic concentration and number of L2 and foreign language speakers are thus two additional criteria of linguistic demography to be reckoned with.

The number of countries where the language is dominant and has de jure or de facto official or national status also counts, in terms of prestige, ease of communication, and reducing trade barriers. In 59 sovereign countries English has official status, Mandarin Chinese in two, three if Taiwan is counted separately (cf. Chapter 7, Table 6). The only non-European language that enjoys official status in a double-digit number of countries is Arabic, which can claim economic utility in the Arabic-speaking world, but not much beyond; for, as its case illustrates, there are still other criteria, such as the GDP of the countries where a language is spoken and the GDP per capita of its speakers. Taken by itself, this criterion makes for a different language ranking, as can be inferred from Table 9 which lists the ten biggest economies and their dominant languages. However, in terms of per capita GDP, English, Chinese, and Arabic are outranked by three languages with extremely small speech communities: Norwegian, Finnish, and Swedish, and also by German, Japanese, and Italian.[13] Regarding English, this is a consequence of its usage in so many countries, including relatively low-GDP countries, such as Burundi, Cameroon, Eswatini, Zambia, and Zimbabwe.

Table 9 Dominant languages of the world's ten biggest economies

Country	GDP 2017 in US$	Population 2017	GDP per capita US$	% of world GDP	De jure or de facto official language
US	19.485 trillion	325,084,756	59,939	24.80	English
China	12.237 trillion	1,421,021,791	8,612	15.12	Mandarin
Japan	4.872 trillion	127,502,725	38,214	6.02	Japanese
Germany	3.693 trillion	82,658,409	44,680	4.56	German
India	2.651 trillion	1,338,676,785	1,980	3.28	Hindi/ English
UK	2.638 trillion	66,727,461	39,532	3.26	English
France	2.583 trillion	64,842,509	39,827	3.19	French
Brazil	2.054 trillion	207,833,823	9,881	2.54	Portuguese
Italy	1.944 trillion	60,673,701	32,038	2.40	Italian
Canada	1.647 trillion	36,732,095	44,841	2.04	English/ French

Source of statistics: Worldometer[14]

Yet another variable to consider is literacy. It tends to be low in low-GDP countries, as indicated in Table 10, which lists the ten countries with the lowest literacy rates: with the exception of Afghanistan, all multilingual African countries.

Table 10 The ten countries with the lowest literacy rates

Country	Literacy rate 2022
Ethiopia	39.0%
Chad	38.0%
Central African Republic	37.0%
Afghanistan	32.0%
Mali	31.0%
Burkina Faso	29.0%
Benin	29.0%
South Sudan	27.0%
Guinea	25.0%
Niger	15.0%

Source: WorldAtlas[15]

The relative wealth of a speech community has a bearing on the attractiveness of its language, and the same holds for the relative level of education. With 342 million L1 speakers, Hindi ranks among the most widely spoken languages on earth,[16] but it is not only geographically concentrated in India, it also has a very high percentage of illiterate speakers, as is shown in Table 11.

Table 11 suggests that there is an inverse relationship between the economic wealth of nations and multilingualism. Actually, it has long been assumed that 'a country that is linguistically highly heterogeneous is always underdeveloped' (Pool 1972: 213). This is corroborated by the fact that the linguistically most diverse countries relative to population size are on the whole poor (Romaine 2009). However, studies in recent years have thrown the assumed causal relationship between national multilingualism and development into doubt. For example, comparing four African countries with four Southeast Asian countries, sociolinguist Paulin Djité (2014) has shown that the latter group is not much better off economically by using their own national languages than the former, which use an ex-colonial language in addition to their many

Table 11 Countries by percentage of world non-literate population

Country	Percentage of world non-literate population	Adult literacy rate	Number of languages
India	33.8%	81.3%	387
China	11.2%	90.9	201
Bangladesh	6.5%	41.1%	38
Pakistan	6.4%	41.5%	69
Nigeria	2.8%	66.8%	505
Ethiopia	2.7%	41.5%	82
Egypt	2.6%	55.6%	10
Indonesia	2.3%	87.9%	726
Brazil	1.9%	88.2%	192

Source: UNESCO 2004. EFA Global Monitoring Report 2005: Education for All—the Quality Imperative.

regional and local languages. The case of Greece and the euro mentioned above shows that a common currency can be more beneficial for some than for others. Looking at anglophone, lusophone, and francophone countries of sub-Sahara Africa, the same can be said of a common language, especially as used in the educational system, although more focussed research on the economic advantages of ex-colonial languages in these countries is necessary (see Chapter 5).

Further, languages differ regarding their domain-specific utility for commerce, work, trade, and as company language; education, as subject or language of instruction; science, for publications, at conferences and for research collaboration; pop culture, religion, tourism, book publication, mass-media, and machine translation software.

All of these domains and functions interact in complex ways, thereby influencing the language choices of individuals, and preferences of groups and governments. That much we know, but it remains difficult to find reliable data that confirm a connection between economic development and the value of a language, however calculated. There are several reasons for this. One is that socio-economic and political configurations keep changing. In the pioneer countries, industrialization arguably required or at least developed along with a certain degree of linguistic unification, so that other countries then also considered this necessary and followed their example. Great social transformations like industrialization or, nowadays, digitization and the transition from material production to knowledge-based economies, even if consciously experienced and deliberately pursued, always have unforeseen consequences and involve unplanned ideological shifts, such as, for instance, the shift in recent decades from an emphasis on homogeneity to diversity in the countries most committed to national linguistic unity. Paradigmatically, the US Association of National Advertisers (ANA) celebrated 'diversity' as the 2021 word of the year,[17] giving expression to a worldwide trend with repercussions for the appreciation of linguistic diversity to which we will turn in Chapters 9 and 10.

Such shifts in attitude make what is difficult to begin with even more difficult, namely the separation of the economic from the ideational value of language. The choice of the language of instruction in elementary schools discussed above (p. 81f.) is a case in point. In developing countries, ex-colonial languages are often chosen for this function because of their perceived economic value as languages of wider communication, while the more indirect economic value of pupils' L1 that may have a small speech community, but generates better learning outcomes, remains hidden from view. Though not traded on the world market, these languages still have value for their speakers. For this reason, UNESCO has been promoting multilingual education and mother-tongue instruction through its language policy for decades.[18] Yet the lure of economic gain associated with languages of wider communication continues to influence language education policies in many developing countries.

In such ways the properties, functions, and rankings of languages interact with socio-economic configurations and policies on local, national, and international levels. If this was not clear all along, the rise of English in the course of the last century has made it clear that there is a world system of languages. No language exists in a vacuum; rather, with their speakers they act on each other vying for territories and domains. De Swaan (2001) conceptualized the global language constellation as a four-tier system. 'Peripheral languages'—his term—are the great majority of all languages spoken by thousands of small communities.

Many of them are oral languages, not written, and hence have no market value. 'Central languages', including many national languages, are used for inter-community communication and are much less numerous than peripheral languages. Still fewer are 'super-central languages'. Often called 'languages of wider communication', they form the third tier which includes no more than a dozen or so languages. And then there is at the top the sole 'hyper-central language', English.

The hyper-central position reflects, and is determined by, above all political-economic factors. The World Economic Forum,[19] which maintains a website in four languages, English, Spanish, Chinese, and Japanese, in 2016 also took an interest in language utility deliberating the question which language would enable an extra-terrestrial visitor to most fully engage with humans (Chan 2016). For this exercise, the author uses five variables to construct a Power Language Index:

1. Geography: the ability to travel.
2. Economy: the ability to participate in an economy.
3. Communication: the ability to engage in dialogue.
4. Knowledge and media: the ability to consume knowledge and media.
5. Diplomacy: the ability to engage in international relations.

Geography, communication, knowledge access and transmission, and diplomacy are paid due attention, but in the end, economy is central. Travel has an economic side, knowledge is valuable, and diplomacy rarely ignores economic interest. The all-important financial market is largely positioned in the West. New York and London playing the dominant role, eight of the world's 10 financial centres are English-speaking/proficient cities, even in Asia. While Tokyo is the capital of a populous, wealthy country, it lags behind the much smaller Hong Kong and Singapore where the English infrastructure is better developed. The global elites rely on English, whose members hailing from non-English-speaking countries are underrepresented. GDP of such countries is lower, as is the number of billionaires, the 'movers and shakers of the world'. As pointed out repeatedly, since language configurations keep changing, rankings are of momentary significance at best. Interestingly, therefore, Chan ventures a mid-century forecast of the Language Power Index ranking, as indicated in Table 12.

Table 12 Power Language Index ranking 2050, according to Chan (2016)

Rank	Language
1	English
2	Mandarin
3	Spanish
4	French
5	Arabic
6	Russian
7	German
8	Portuguese
9	Hindi
10	Japanese

No surprise that English is still 'hyper-central', and that the ex-colonial languages English, Spanish, French, and Portuguese are still among the top ten. More striking is the prediction that Mandarin will be number two, and the inclusion of Hindi on the list many will not consider a matter of course either. Whatever the veracity of this forecast, it highlights the fact that language hierarchies are not hewn in stone and draws our attention to the historicity of the contemporary world order of languages and how it is influenced by economic developments. It is also worth noting that if our purpose, or thought experiment, weren't to 'most fully engage with humans', a different ranking would likely result.

Economics of language and language policy

If, as emerges from the previous sections, language is an element of the economic process, what does this imply for language policy? In particular, what lessons can be drawn from economically informed rankings of languages? Such rankings are indicative of the utility value of languages. Considering foreign language education, which in many countries is a field of political responsibility (acquisition planning), the economic impact is evident. In the previous chapter we have seen that some wealthy countries maintain elaborate institutional structures for the promotion of their national languages abroad, to a large extent for economic reasons. At the same time, the foreign language education landscape at home has been changing, also for economic reasons, as in many countries English has become the first and often only foreign language of school education. This development runs counter to long-established language education policies, as, for example, the traditionally strong modern foreign language education system in the Netherlands. A recent study describes the decline of foreign language education provisions and skills on all levels in the face of the unabated advance of English which 'some consider no longer to be a foreign language in the Netherlands' (Michel, Vidon, de Graaff, and Lowie 2020). The authors see this market-driven development as detrimental to public interest and in turn underpin their argument with economic considerations:

> Many initiatives from within education— supported by calls from businesses representatives trading with the neighbouring countries—will lead to a more prosperous status of modern foreign languages in the future. In particular, the new Dutch curriculum (curriculum.nu) may induce policy decisions based on insights, expertise and experience of teacher education programmes and research. A changing world, where the Anglo-Saxon ideal suffers from Brexit and the US' focus on themselves, may be a wake-up call for Dutch policy makers. The Dutch owe their younger generations to train them in 21st century skills including multiple modern foreign languages, as is advocated by the EU (ibid.).

The Council of Europe, too, embraces multilingualism and maintains a language policy which covers foreign languages, major languages of schooling, languages spoken in the family, and minority or regional languages.[20] The linguistic integration of migrants and refugees, which is important both for human resource management and social participation, has been one of its major concerns for the past half century. Despite these policies and the emphasis on linguistic multitude for the Council of Europe's 'core values', the dominance of English in the council's activities is no less than in the EU.

Prior to Brexit, the EU has resisted the economic pressure to adopt English as its official or working language and is more unlikely to do so after.[21] However, since education is subject to national sovereignty, the EU is powerless to enforce its language policy recommendations to make the citizens of its member states competent in at least two foreign languages. The Netherlands is not the only country where other foreign languages have lost ground to hyper-central English. In the neoliberal world, ruled by the imperatives of competition, capital accumulation, and profit maximization, it is becoming increasingly difficult to carve out niches of activities and values not dominated by market forces. This can also be seen as the downside of ranking languages or the universality of ranking as such, which has invaded not only language policy, but policy decision making in general.

A 2016 report commissioned by the European Parliament's Committee on Culture and Education notes that the current lack of attention of EU language policy towards multilingualism is not justified and applies economic reasoning to back up its criticism:

> The European Strategy for Multilingualism (ESM) has three general socio-economic objectives, namely, strengthening social cohesion, the integration of migrants, and intercultural dialogue; promoting mobility of the labour force in the Single Market, employability and growth in Europe; managing in an effective and inclusive way multilingual communication in a supranational democracy.[22]

This report by political scientist Vicente Climent-Ferrando (2023) has analysed the EU's policy response to these appeals by means of the policy cycle model cited at the end of Chapter 1. Published in English only, the report reviews the multilingualism policy of the EU in terms of cost and benefits regarding mobility and employability, promoting integration of migrants, effects on individual income, contributions to GDP and trade, and managing multilingual institutions. It shows that regional and minority languages are largely excluded from these policy initiatives. It documents international conferences on multilingualism and language learning organized by the European Commission, for example with the government of India in 2008 and the government of China in 2011.

In addition, it provides an in-depth and very useful overview of the EU's many initiatives to promote multilingualism, but it does not offer much advice on what policies the EU could or should adopt in relation to English: submit to market forces or develop policies to regulate its function within the community.

To conclude, in this chapter we have looked at facets of languages as a means of exchange, as common goods, as human capital and a factor of employability, investment with variable rates of return, trade barrier, and contribution to GDP. The questions of how they influence language policy and if or how language policy objectives have to be adjusted when they are at odds with cost efficiency and other language market forces are critical for our understanding of the design and implementation of language policy, but they cannot be answered uniformly. The main reasons for this are two. One, socio-political and language configurations in economically advanced countries of the global north and the countries of the global south are very different; and two, decolonization, deregulation, and globalization have changed global language configurations to which especially affluent countries of the north have to adjust, as will be discussed in more detail in the following chapter.

Further reading

Chan, Kai. 2016. These Are the Most Powerful Languages in the World. *World Economic Forum*, 2 December. https://www.weforum.org/agenda/2016/12/these-are-the-most-powerful-languages-in-the-world/

Coulmas, Florian. 2009. Language and Economy. In Li Wei (ed.) Contemporary Applied Linguistics, Volume 2 Linguistics for the Real World. New York: Continuum, 28–45.

Gazzola, Michele and Bengt-Arne Wickström (eds.). 2016. *The Economics of Language Policy*. Cambridge, Massachusetts: MIT Press.

Grin, François, Claudio Sfreddo, François Vaillancourt. 2010. *The Economics of the Multilingual Workplace*. London: Routledge.

Kirschner, Jonathan. 2003. Money is politics. *Review of International Political Economy* 10: 645–660.

9

The new multitude—migration, language, and citizenship

> Gérald Darmanin veut conditionner la carte de séjour à la maîtrise d'un niveau minimal de français
>
> Le ministre de l'Intérieur Gérald Darmanin souhaiterait conditionner la délivrance de titres de séjour aux étrangers à leur maîtrise de la langue française.
>
> Le gouvernement va proposer de conditionner la délivrance de la carte de séjour pluriannuelle (CSP) à la maîtrise d'un niveau minimal de français afin de conforter l'intégration, a annoncé ce mardi 12 juillet le ministre de l'Intérieur Gérald Darmanin.[1]

If state authority over language is undermined by commercial interest, as we have seen in the previous chapter, it also comes under pressure by accelerated population movements. Progressing urbanization, concurrent with quantitative changes in population distribution, has transformed mainly rural into mainly urban societies around the world for more than a century, and since the end of World War II, under the impact of decolonization, reconstruction, and then globalization, many European nation states have become more similar to typical immigrant countries like Australia, Canada, and the United States. The former colonial powers Belgium, Britain, France, Netherlands, Portugal, and Spain have attracted substantial immigration from their former colonies, while Germany, Austria, Switzerland, and the Scandinavian countries

Language Policy. Florian Coulmas, Oxford University Press. © Florian Coulmas (2025).
DOI: 10.1093/9780191976377.003.0009

recruited migrant labour from Turkey and Morocco, among others. In addition, a continuous stream of refugees, on land routes from Asian countries and across the Mediterranean from sub-Saharan countries, have contributed to changing the demographic composition of Italy and other southern European countries. Because of the development and wealth gap between the global north and south, this is a continuing dynamic, as recent figures on citizenship acquisition in five European countries illustrate (Table 13). Figures of settlement permits would be considerably higher, and because of freedom of movement within the EU since 2004, some demographic shifts—how many people from Eastern European EU member states are working in the Netherlands, Germany, and Belgium, for example—are statistically hard to grasp. Migration push from the south is complemented by demographically caused pull in the north, that is, by social ageing which has turned even Japan into a labour import country, as 10 per cent of its population are now (2024) 80 years or older. Immigration alleviates the unwelcome effects of social ageing in two ways. It helps to reduce labour shortage, especially in the care sector, and, since most immigrants are relatively young, by slowing down population ageing curbs the old-age dependency ratio.

Table 13 Citizenship acquisitions in select European countries[2]

Country	Number of citizenship acquisitions
France, 2021	130,000
Germany, 2021	131,600
Italy, 2021	131,800
Netherlands, 2020	56,000
United Kingdom, 2021	190,175

The interplay of population ageing and immigration in developed countries is a highly multifaceted process which happens as the world is getting more crowded, the eight-billionth 'world citizen' just having been born.[3] The ongoing social, economic, and political changes underlying this macro-transformation affect most every part of our life. Our focus here is on the linguistic consequences and what they imply for language policy. Within a couple of generations, migration has turned many cities in the northern hemisphere into multilingual environments where dozens if not hundreds of languages are spoken, with many implications for municipal and national institutions. More apt would be to say the language multitude that had always marked cities has been amplified by immigration and turned into a political issue. The multilingualism of a multi-ethnic population poses challenges not just for language education policy, but also for public services and courts of law, among others, in a way that once again raises the political question of how to balance heterogeneity and homogeneity, inclusion of difference and assimilation.

The public sphere and the nation state

The changes just mentioned were fast, but they did not happen overnight, and possible policy responses start from established language configurations. In Europe, the national language ideology, though not very old, has done much to make the unity of nation and state look like inevitable destiny and linguistic homogeneity the default. It is perceived by many not as historically contingent but as a necessity of modern life around which highly elaborate intellectual edifices have been built, notably the idea of the public sphere. This concept was introduced by Jürgen Habermas in the 1960s and then became an important topic in discussions about relations between state and society throughout the Western world. It refers to a realm of social life where information of general rather than personal interest can be exchanged and a public opinion thus be formed, where citizens engage in rational debate on behalf of the common good. It is accessible by all citizens who are guaranteed freedom of assembly and association and the freedom to communicate with each other in speech and writing. In contrast to the absolutist state, well characterized by the apocryphal remark *L'État, c'est moi* attributed to Louis XIV, the modern state includes a social ambit that mediates between state and society to make democratic control of state activities possible, the 'public sphere'. At the time when it became an important political concept, newspapers, magazines, radio, and television were the media of the manifestation of the public sphere—which was tacitly assumed to be monolingual, although this was never a topic much discussed in this connection.[4] Print capitalism, as described by Benedict Anderson (see p. 58) had brought about some degree of linguistic unification in European states, making this assumption relatively plausible for scholars who had themselves grown up in societies that used the same language for school education, public administration, and the military, which led to what Indian linguist Debi Prasanna Pattanayak (1998: 132) described as 'blindness to diversity'.

Two important changes have taken place since: the multilingualization of Western societies and the penetration of social media into all sectors of society. Many cities are now places where people from various parts of the world have come together to interact with each other, and people almost everywhere for the first time in human history are able to instantly interact with people in other parts of the world. The nation state today has to adapt to both of these ongoing processes; for the public sphere as originally conceived in Habermas' historical account was a *national* sphere, much like print capitalism was national capitalism. Sue Wright (2015) has characterized the view of the world as a mosaic of stable national monolingualisms grounded in this conception as outdated. She rightly argues that globalization forces us to recognize a more complex picture of communities of communication in a highly diverse world. Some of the differences which thus appear between the public sphere of print capitalism and the supra-public sphere of web capitalism are tentatively summarized in Table 14.

Language and citizenship

If the just mentioned changes that distinguish the public sphere of print capitalism from the supra-public sphere of web capitalism are indeed significant, the question is whether mass migration and wireless mobile communication technologies have created a global,

Table 14 Select characteristics of print capitalism and web capitalism

Print capitalism	Web capitalism
• Homogenization	• Pluralization
• Nationalism	• Human rights
• Uniformity	• Diversity
• Industrialism/conformism	• Customization/individualism
• Maximize print run	• Print on demand
• Language standard/standard language	• Language multitude/dialect revival
• Monolingual mindset	• Multilingualism/multiculturalism

cosmopolitan sphere. The rise of multilingual cities over recent decades in nominally unilingual countries is beyond doubt. Never before had so many migrants from other countries and continents settled in cities around the world to form ethnolinguistic communities. To what extent does this development challenge the congruence of nationality and state, of cultural and political community? More specifically, what are the implications for residence, citizenship, and naturalization? The multiplicity of ethnolinguistic communities in most advanced industrial countries makes a return to the culturally and linguistically uniform nation state unrealistic—if it could be anything more than a fictitious return. Some governments, nevertheless, adhere to this vision and adopt language policies to this end, as the example mentioned at the beginning of this chapter shows. Because of the multiplicity of migrant communities, ethnolinguistically motivated secession is equally unrealistic. Nevertheless, it must be acknowledged that the nation state as a model of state and administrative structures appropriate to self-determined autonomous political action has come under pressure, as minority protection and legitimate claims of political action by sub-national actors have become policy issues (Loring and Ramanthan 2016).

In the modern nation state, language plays an important role beyond the ideologization of the national language as the 'spirit' or the 'mirror of the nation' or the symbol of belonging and national identity. It is the medium of a huge literature, laws, regulations, and legal action proceedings, most government documents, tax forms, permits, ID papers, job advertisements, and many more papers which are considered indispensable for social and political participation. This is what made the public sphere so important for modern societies and for the emergence of democratic states. Equality of human dignity is the foundation which nowadays is put to the test by the fact that most modern societies are characterized by some degree of diversity of race, religion, culture, and language. What do we do when actual equality requires not just access to, but also basic comprehension of, state manifestations coded in the national language and where a growing part of the population does not fulfil this requirement? This is one of the critical questions for language policy in the present time.

Language tests

It is useful in this connection to recall the language policy of the EU. The most conspicuous feature of this great experiment to create a modern supranational polity that makes national identities and a European identity compatible is that its members were unable to agree on a common language. This shows among other things how deeply rooted the nation state is in Europe and the national language with it. Now that the status of the national language is being challenged from below—by local communities—rather than from above—by European supranational structures—the same attachment to the national language makes itself felt by limiting the pluralism of modern multi-ethnic societies. The very idea of a nation state implies limiting pluralism by drawing physical and conceptual boundaries with regard to who does and who does not belong. Here, language can, but does not necessarily have to, serve as a criterion. Since the turn of the century, we have witnessed an intensification of employing language for this purpose, which is particularly evident in language testing for naturalization.

In response to increasing immigration in the last three decades, testing proficiency in the national language has become an integral part of the language policy of many immigrant recipient countries. In the 1990s, language testing was only a prerequisite for citizenship acquisition through naturalization in exceptional cases, but has since gradually been embraced by a growing number of countries and extended beyond citizenship acquisition to residence permission (Council of Europe 2014). By the 2020s, it had become the rule. This can be understood as a measure to ensure that all new members of society are able to understand their rights and duties and communicate with the government. It can also be understood as an exclusionary policy committed to obsolete concepts of nationality, ethnicity, and monolingualism. These two opposing perspectives make for an intensification of political discourse about immigration, inclusion, and the compatibility of boundaries with human rights.[5]

That national governments of democratic states place importance on their citizens' ability to communicate with them looks like a matter of course, but the issue is more complicated than it seems at first sight. Think of persons born and raised abroad who have inherited their citizenship, but have acquired no or only limited competency in their 'native' language. That they will not be subjected to a language test when they decide to settle in the country of their parents is just one example of the discriminatory aspects of an integration policy that requires proficiency in the national language. Or consider refugees and asylum seekers, that is, persons on the move to escape from war—at the time of writing close to 8 million refugees from Ukraine in the EU—hunger, or other calamities. They too do not have to take language tests, but these persons are not always easily distinguished from other groups.

More generally, who is entitled to full citizenship is a hazy issue, which current crises and long-term demographic developments do not make easier. Traditional models of citizenship are two, *ius sanguinis*, citizenship by descent, as just mentioned, and *ius soli*, citizenship through place of birth (by a legally resident mother). In the wake of migration flows in recent decades, two changes regarding the acquisition of citizenship could be observed in many host countries of migrants: naturalization after several years of residence and the possibility of dual citizenship. A majority of the 27 EU member states now allow dual citizenship (Germany, Greece, France, Ireland, Cyprus, Czech Republic, Denmark, Finland, Hungary, Italy, Latvia, Lithuania, Malta, Portugal, Spain, Poland, Sweden). Addressing potential applicants, the EU informs about language testing in a rather low-key way: 'Naturalization usually requires being able to prove a certain level of local language proficiency.'[6] This provision, however, does not apply to a large number of people, namely nationals of EU member states. Because of freedom of movement within the EU there is no need for them to apply for citizenship in another EU country where they work or reside for other reasons, and they do not therefore count as migrants, who are understood to be non-EU nationals.[7] Which in turn means that a large part of the linguistic multitude, especially in western European countries, develops under the radar and is ignored in the context of language assessment for immigration. On the other hand, language testing has become increasingly important for non-EU nationals seeking naturalization or permanent residence permission. Because the stakes are high, the validity, fairness, and meaningfulness of language assessment is intensely discussed as a political instrument of regulating immigration along lines that are neither objective nor universally accepted. However, for the time being language testing for integration is a part of EU language policy.[8]

Cosmopolis, ethnopolis, online-polis

While the continuing importance of the national language for political organization is indisputable, technology comes into play in ways no one could have imagined when the national language ideology evolved. As this idea took root, citizens became what for the sake of argument we may call 'prisoners of the national language'. Whatever political action you wanted to engage in, whatever communication with the state you wanted to have, it had to be done in the garment of the national language—until the arrival of 'technologies of freedom', the title of a book in which the late political scientist Ithiel de Sola Pool (1983) attempted very early on to envision the benefits of new communication technologies. Whether the optimism expressed by the title was justified is still a matter of heated debate between those who hail technological innovations as means of enhancing liberty and those who see it tilt to new forms of tyranny, but that a communications revolution has occurred few would deny. And it is not just a matter of replacing typewriters with computers and cables with wireless connections, but one that transforms society. Exploring, even superficially, the changes that were brought about and are still going on goes far beyond the limits of this book, which can only mention some implications for language policy.

Let us again take a look at immigration. Poor as they may be, the great majority of migrants and refugees nowadays have a smartphone, because it is an indispensable tool for them to pursue their migratory journeys. It not only allows them to stay in touch with friends and family, they also employ it to gather information about safe routes and barriers, to contact authorities and to communicate with medical services, among others. According to the UN Refugee Agency, migrants and refugees use social media platforms in 'five primary ways—communication, translation, information, navigation and representation.'[9] Communication includes contacts with underground networks which in many cases are involved in organizing and executing their journeys. Needless to say, recipient countries spend many resources to find and disable these networks which, thanks to the technology on which they are built, remain active after the journey. Smartphones are not only useful in transit, but are valuable in many ways after arrival, if such is accomplished.

The ways in which this particular population of migrants and refugees use their electronic devices are unique when they are on the move, but also represent many of the changes that online communication technologies have brought about in society at large. And these changes have taught us that the internet hasn't just brought us freedom and other good things, as Sola Pool would probably agree today. It has undermined the public sphere as a realm of communicative rationality by opening the floodgates to disinformation, the spread of conspiracy theories, online stalking, hate mail, 'alternative facts/news', ransomware, and new crimes that didn't exist just a few decades ago. The freedom-supporting forces sponsoring anti-government protests through social media are counterbalanced by government campaigns of propaganda and deception, and aggressive media manipulation campaigns are by no means limited to autocratic regimes.

Looking at migration brings yet two other aspects of the digital turn into focus: ubiquitous monitoring and multilingualism. Under pressure of both commercial and governmental interests, the public sphere has become a sphere of advertisement and mass surveillance—in autocratic countries and liberal democracies. Through a variety of crime prevention and law enforcement laws and programmes, governments have built personal data collection or interception networks that are tighter than ever, and private companies are using every imaginable method to exploit personal data to advance their products. In combination with the ubiquitous excessive stream of information, these uses of the internet have hollowed out the function of the public sphere for controlling state action. At the same time, digital technologies have altered the nature of the public sphere by opening it up to a much larger 'public', sidelining gatekeepers such as publishers, editors, and proprietors of media, and by enabling the use of other languages. Migrants and refugees reinforce a more comprehensive trend by bringing in additional linguistic resources, or language impediments, however you choose to look at it. They speak other languages and often have insufficient command of the dominant language of the host country. When communicating with public bodies, they often use automatic translation, effectively, it should be added, because in the last twenty years these programmes by public and private suppliers have made spectacular progress.

Can this technically enlarged communicative competence be applied in elections? This is too general a question, however, within the EU it may well be useful for citizens with limited command of the dominant language of their country of residence, for 'every citizen of the Union has the right to vote and to stand as a candidate at municipal elections in the EU country in which he or she resides under the same conditions as nationals of that country', as is stipulated in Article 40 of the EU Charter of Fundamental Rights.[10] This does not apply to national elections, but on local levels competence in the national language is no prerequisite of making use of your right to vote. While the number of actual cases will be limited, as a matter of principle regarding the link between language, public sphere and democracy, respect for diversity and active citizenship, this regulation for EU citizens is quite interesting. Cities with substantial populations with a migration background are found throughout Europe, and the number of majority-minority cities, i.e., cities where social, national, ethnic, or racial minorities make up more than half the population, is increasing. Minorities have always been a problem for democratic governance, but what becomes of the imperative of equality when they constitute the majority is an even hairier question.

In the cosmopolis of pre-digital ages speakers of different languages were nothing remarkable; however, transnational demographic movements have grown significantly since. In 2020, an estimated 281 million people were living in a country other than their countries of birth, 128 million more than in 1990.[11] Increased international mobility and digital technology have made multilingualism a much wider aspect of social life not just in big urban centres but in many small and middle-sized towns (some examples being listed in Table 15) where migrants have settled and formed ethnic communities and which are now characterized by the copresence of ethnicities, cultures, languages, religions, and social strata that have to accommodate and find ways of living together. Because cosmopolitanism has often been portrayed as an elitist ideology entertained by intellectuals who can afford it (e.g., Sassen 2010), the cosmopolis is now sometimes called 'ethnopolis', which is more than a change of name. The cosmopolitan accepts and accommodates to diversity without making it a big issue. In the ethnopolis the separation of difference—often emphasized as 'identities'—is more pronounced as members of ethnic groups are segregated by forced ghettoization or voluntarily built diaspora communities (Sheffer 2003). Nevertheless, the new multitude is mobile and multilingual. Mobility means that the members of these communities have experienced language contact moving back and forth between the languages spoken at home and outside, in school, at the work place, in civic administrations, and by other ethnic groups. They have also experienced the deterritorialization of their L1 which is spoken in the country of their/their antecedents' origin as well as in their neighbourhood. In sociolinguistics, urban multilingualism has therefore become a critical research field dealing with new contact varieties that emerge at the intersection of social class and ethnicity. For language policy it implies new challenges with regard to education, administration, and social integration.

Because of considerable regional differences in the multilingualization of societies these challenges are not necessarily met at the national level. The role migrant languages are supposed to play for social integration also varies from country to country. Some countries adopted

Table 15 Select small and mid-sized EU cities with high migrant background population[12]

City, country	Population 2020/2021	Migration background
Antwerp, Belgium	506,000	50%
Bielefeld, Germany	334,000	39%
Eindhoven, Netherlands	238,000	40%
Galway, Ireland	80,000	26%
Linz, Austria	203,000	25%
Prato, Italy	192,000	25%
Torrevieja, Spain	83,000	48%

assimilationist policies whereby immigrants are expected to learn the dominant language, while scarce attention is paid to the languages they are bringing with them, France traditionally having been the paradigm example of this model of integration. Others such as the Netherlands and most anglophone countries more readily accept the reshaping of the national linguistic space and have embraced linguistic diversity and multiculturalism as a philosophy steering inclusion rather than assimilation. Both migrants' maintenance of their ethnic language by means of online communication and the fact that migration today is no longer necessarily a one-way move have reinforced the multiculturalist model of migrant reception. Increased mobility has made return migration more common, which has repercussions for LP, both on the level of educational institutions and family language policy. Because temporary labour migration and return migration are perceived as individual responsibility, maintenance and development of L1 among migrants' offspring has become the central issue of family language policy.[13]

Prospects

To sum up, the diversification of urban spaces is a fact of life. Whether the ethnopolis that has been transformed so profoundly in the last decades has become the exemplary place of recognizing diversity as essential to the human condition (e.g., de Souza 2022) or as a threat to democracy (e.g., Keen 2015) must remain an open question, because we cannot dissociate it from worldviews and preferences. What can be said is that, given the crucial function of language for social life, language policy must play a role in this, be it to support language maintenance on the part of migrants, if they so desire, or to help them acquire full competence in the dominant language, or both. Currently, strong contrasts between acceptance and rejection of migrants can be observed in the populations of many Western countries. Whichever gains the upper hand will likely influence governments' language policies, as evidenced by the initiatives mentioned at the beginning of this chapter and Chapter 5.

The expansion of the public sphere into cyberspace likewise is a fact of life. The genie of digital communication technologies cannot be put back in the bottle. Migrants have shown that these tools have added a new dimension to social multilingualism which is why they are sometimes called 'digital cosmopolitans' (Zuckerman 2013). Whether this will contribute to respect for diversity and to democratic participation or have the opposite effect is once again a question which is to be answered by societies as they evolve and come to terms with new realities. What can and needs to be done is building a language policy for cyberspace. Policies are limited to national spaces or may be subject to international treaties. Jurisdiction in cyberspace does not fit in well and therefore is one of the overriding issues in evolving international law. Policy is not law, but it can influence legislation which is dearly needed, since online technologies continue to evolve and legal frameworks are struggling to keep up.

What does freedom of expression in cyberspace mean at present, what should it mean in the future, and who should be held responsible for transgressions? If there should be policing and cleaning up of the internet, who should be charged with it? Should such regulations apply to all languages, and if not, will languages be selected on pragmatic or on principled grounds? These are just some of the questions pending answers.

Where we are today, we have to acknowledge that digitization and mass migration have profoundly transformed communication in urban and cyberspace and thus changed the world. The great wave of diversification that has swept across the globe has, among other things, brought with it an increasing recognition of minority languages, which in the context of modernist national language regimes were largely ignored. Nevertheless, many problems pertaining to language policy remain, among them the future of the world's 'endangered languages', as they have come to be called, in train with nation building and the spread of Western civilization around the world. The language policy challenges that emerged in this context on national and international levels in recent decades are the subject of the next chapter.

Further reading

Capstick, Tony. 2020. *Language and Migration*. London: Routledge.

Extra, Guus, Massimiliano Spotti, and Piet Van Avermaet (eds.) 2009. *Language Testing, Migration and Citizenship: Cross-national Perspectives on Integration Regimes*. London: Continuum.

Kymlicka, Will. 2007. *Multicultural Odysseys: Navigating the New International Politics of Diversity*. Oxford: Oxford University Press.

Laitin, David D. 2000. What is a language community? *American Journal of Political Science* 44, 142–155.

10

Linguistic rights

Language endangerment as a political issue

> The European Charter for Regional or Minority Languages (ECRML) is the European convention for the protection and promotion of languages used by traditional minorities. Together with the Framework Convention for the Protection of National Minorities it constitutes the Council of Europe's commitment to the protection of national minorities. The implementation of the Charter is monitored by a committee of independent experts.[1]
>
> The ECRMLanguages was opened for signature on 5 November 1992. It came into force five and a half years later, on 1 March 1998.—What took the Europeans so long?
>
> Each State Party to the present Covenant undertakes to respect and to ensure to all individuals within its territory and subject to its jurisdiction the rights recognized in the present Covenant, without distinction of any kind, such as race, colour, sex, language, religion, political or other opinion, national or social origin, property, birth or other status.[2]

To reflect the contemporary popularity of diversity and support to small ethnic communities that have been repressed, marginalized or, if lucky, ignored during modernization, UNESCO declared 2019 the 'International Year of Indigenous Languages'. By so doing it prepared the way for the United Nations General Assembly (Resolution

Language Policy. Florian Coulmas, Oxford University Press. © Florian Coulmas (2025).
DOI: 10.1093/9780191976377.003.0010

A/RES/74/135) to proclaim the period between 2022 and 2032 as the 'International Decade of Indigenous Languages' (IDIL 2022–2032). In recent decades, awareness of the problems faced by speakers of small languages has clearly increased significantly, and scholars who study such languages and campaign for them to gain attention are unlikely to be condescendingly smiled at, as only a century ago they were.[3] Declarations and resolutions of this sort needn't be more than reassuring symbolic tokens, however, the initiatives by UNESCO and the UN General Assembly make it clear that small languages have indeed become a political issue.

The situation

As mentioned occasionally in previous chapters, the languages of the world are numbered in the thousands, with 7,100 being a widely cited figure. As languages are constantly changing, embedded in evolving socio-economic systems, among them there are those that have recently fallen into disuse or are about to do so, varieties that are vying for language status and others merging with one another. Accordingly, there is a degree of uncertainty about such figures, but whatever the categories applied to counting languages, it is obvious that groups whose speech others cannot understand outnumber sovereign states by a factor of 35 or more. Accordingly, since the linguistically unitary state is the rare exception, if it exists at all, language minorities are potentially on the political agenda of all states, which does not imply that linguistic diversity is evenly distributed.

Another point already mentioned in Chapter 6 is that among the languages of the world there is an inverse relationship between populous and small communities of speakers. This is a fact that wasn't widely known a hundred years ago or, if it was, not a matter of concern in a world where not much more than 20 per cent of the population were literate, proper languages had a written code and those that didn't were dialects, patois, jargons, or, at best, primitive languages and as such were not worthy of protection. All of this has changed. Linguists have spread awareness of the difference between writing and language (although confusion can still be encountered in the media), and that unwritten languages can be structurally as complex and fascinating testimonies to the creativity of the human mind as written ones. Considering the well-documented fact that most European languages acquired a written form only a few centuries ago, this shouldn't be a pathbreaking insight, but memory is short. Moreover, the discourse on 'primitive' languages is grounded in Eurocentric racism and thus out of fashion, at least in academia (Mazzon 2022)—which brings us another step closer to language policy.

That the 'primitive' languages of times past we now call 'Indigenous' languages is itself a language policy issue of the kind to be deliberated in more detail in the next chapter. At this point, suffice it to say that *primitive* languages were a handicap of which those afflicted had to be relieved by having a civilized tongue, i.e., a European colonial language, imposed upon them, whereas *Indigenous* languages are a valuable intangible heritage of humanity. In brief, this is the story of this ideological transformation.

The division of humanity into speech communities that cannot understand each other has often been seen as a curse, a divine punishment for their sinful hubris. Meanwhile, the view that the multiplicity of languages is a precious asset threatened by Western economic, military, and technological expansion has gained the upper hand. Since the 1990s, the notion of linguistic human rights has become an ideological base that informs discussions and research projects about multilingualism (see, e.g., Ricento 2000; Skutnabb-Kangas and Phillipson 1995, 2023). As the disappearance of languages has accelerated over the last hundred years, and our sensibility to it has increased, terms such as 'endangered languages' and 'language death'[4] have entered the discourse about power structures and languages. This development, as suggested by the inherent metaphor, has been likened to the endangerment of biodiversity (Sutherland 2003, cf. Chapter 4, above). While the parallel between linguistic and biological multitude is intuitively persuasive, since both have come under pressure by similar global developments, the fundamental difference between the reproduction of languages and natural species is obscured by it. Languages cannot die because they don't live. They are artefacts adapted to exigencies on a daily basis and handed down in like manner from one generation to the next. Their speakers can die or decide, voluntarily or forced by circumstances, not to make their offspring continue the linguistic tradition of their forebears. Natural species are never in a situation like that. Furthermore, it is an open question whether the value of the diversity of languages for life on this planet is really comparable with that of natural species. Those who believe in translation—something that does not exist in the natural world—and who know that life in francophone France, Quebec, and Madagascar, for example, is quite different, may have doubts about that. But, whatever the answer, the multiplicity of languages is today considered a precious human legacy deserving to be protected, and the fact that many people around the world believe that loss of languages should be avoided may be sufficient reason in itself to take action accordingly.

Using a variety of predictor variables including demographic shifts, legal recognition, documentation, education policy, socio-economic indicators, and environmental features, a recent study predicts that some 1,500 of the world's languages will no longer be in use by the end of the century (Bromham et al. 2022). More pessimistic assessments see 40 per cent of all languages facing obliteration,[5] and the Universal Declaration of Linguistic Rights, promoted in 1996 by a number of organizations in Barcelona, even believes that 'during the XXI century, 80% of the languages from all over the world may disappear'.[6] Whatever the accuracy of these predictions and warnings, they have a strategic function of directing attention to language minority protection.

Minority protection

In view of such projections, the UN's IDIL 2022–2032 was proclaimed for exactly that purpose, that is, in order to confront language endangerment on international and national levels (Bromham et al. 2022). Documentation is crucial because without it no effective policies can be designed. A major documentation project was UNESCO's Atlas of the World's Languages in Danger of 2010[7] which is waiting to be updated. It shows where communities of declining or endangered languages are concentrated. This is not necessarily in developing or poor countries, although it can be said that socio-economic development has been and still is a major cause of the decline of Indigenous languages, which many of their own speakers consider useless in a (post-)modern interconnected world. For example, the great majority of the languages of the 574 tribes recognized in the United States[8] have ceased to exist or will have no speakers left within a few decades. Poor countries are lagging behind in this regard, as in others, but cannot, and are less inclined to, spend resources for bilingual education and other programmes that might support maintenance of minority languages.

UNESCO explains the purpose of IDIL 2022–2032 as follows:

> [It] aims at ensuring indigenous peoples' right to preserve, revitalize and promote their languages, and mainstreaming linguistic diversity and multilingualism aspects into the sustainable development efforts. It offers a unique opportunity to collaborate in the areas of policy development and stimulate a global dialogue in a true spirit of multistakeholder engagement, and to take necessary measures for the usage, preservation, revitalization and promotion of indigenous languages around the world.[9]

An important notion here is 'indigenous peoples' *right* to preserve, revitalize and promote their languages'. National legal frameworks, constitutions, and laws do not necessarily encompass such a right, but that the most widely recognized international bodies publicly endorse it suggests that it derives not from national or international law but from universal postulates relating to the human condition, as are enshrined in the International Covenant on Civil and Political Rights of 1966, which repeatedly mentions language along with race, skin colour, sex, religion, political or other opinion, national or social origin, property, birth or other status as a criterion that does not allow discrimination of any kind.[10]

For instance, Article 14, 3 which deals with equality of all persons before courts and tribunals stipulates:

> In the determination of any criminal charge against him, everyone shall be entitled to the following minimum guarantees, in full equality: (a) To be informed promptly and in detail in a language which he understands of the nature and cause of the charge against him.

Obviously, a language which he/she understands is not necessarily an Indigenous or other minority language. More significantly, therefore, Article 27 sets an explicit norm for the protection of linguistic minorities:

> In those States in which ethnic, religious or linguistic minorities exist, persons belonging to such minorities shall not be denied the right, in community with the other members of their group, to enjoy their own culture, to profess and practise their own religion, or to use their own language.

Although the covenant was adopted a half a century ago—it entered into force in 1976—its language-related provisions have been transposed into national law in few cases only, in Finland, for example, where 'according to the Constitution, the Sami, as an indigenous people, as well as the Roma and other groups, have the right to maintain and develop their own language and culture'.[11]

Where such a right is recognized, how it is to be implemented and what obligations for the state it implies is a matter of intense debate even among liberal democracies.

Policies of minority protection first took shape in Europe where, after the national languages had been cultivated for a long time at the expense of minority languages, the idea that this is unjust gained some recognition not only in minority groups. A politically important statement in this regard is the Charter for Regional or Minority Languages the Council of Europe adopted in 1992 and which went into force in 1998, as cited at the outset of this chapter. It exemplifies the political and legal intricacies of a language regime that guarantees the protection of minorities. First of all, there is the need to define what is or counts as a minority language, since the languages spoken in a state territory are of various kinds. They may be Indigenous languages—Scottish Gaelic in Scotland; languages of neighbouring countries—French in Italy (*français valdôtain*); languages of 'returned' migrant groups—Russian in Germany; languages of diaspora communities—Chinese in Italy; or sign languages vying for recognition, for instance, in Japan (Mori and Sugimoto 2019). The charter is not designed to encompass all of these languages and therefore states in Article 1 that 'regional and minority languages' do not include 'dialects of the official language(s) of the State or the languages of migrants'.[12] This is a very significant limitation given that the difference between language and dialect may be politically contested, and given that 8.4 per cent of all EU inhabitants were born outside Europe forming numerous ethnolinguistic groups.[13] What is more, the charter has not eliminated the privileged status of the national language. Opinions still differ on how this can be reconciled with the supreme principle of equality in democratic states in times of continuing immigration.

Whose linguistic rights?

It is worth noting in this connection that at the time when the Charter for Regional or Minority Languages was adopted, France did not join the 25 European signatory states and decided to make French by constitutional amendment 'the language of the Republic' (Oakes 2017: 377). Since during the past three centuries few other languages have been as intensely cultivated under state auspices and gained general acceptance as national language, the question is inescapable why such an amendment should have been necessary. Most probably in order to stem the unwelcome tide of other languages entering the public domain through immigration, e.g., Arabic, as well as internal minority languages gaining recognition, e.g., Corsican.

France is a model case here, since the question of how to deal with regional and other minority languages—patois—has been in the background of political discussions, especially about education, since the French Revolution. A critical concept in this connection is again that of linguistic rights. UNESCO's explanatory text about IDIL 2022–2032 speaks of 'indigenous peoples' right to preserve, revitalize and promote their languages', from which it might be inferred that this right is held by groups. Article 27 of the International Covenant on Civil and Political Rights, also quoted above, says that 'persons belonging to such minorities shall not be denied the right, in community with the other members of their group, to enjoy their own culture'. This phrase could be interpreted either way, the right-holders being individual persons or communities. The position of minority languages on the level of the nation state and their significance for citizenship has for the last three decades been the subject of debates in political theory where advocates and opponents of multiculturalism occupy two opposing standpoints.

To cite a third example already mentioned above (p. 158), Finland, being officially bilingual Finnish-Swedish, has a Language Act with detailed provisions for linguistic rights in education, municipal administration, court procedures, among others. The implementation and application of the Language Act is monitored by the Ministry of Justice which makes it clear that '[l]inguistic rights are rights of the individual'.[14] The implication of this statement is that linguistic rights are *not* group rights. A legal system can accord rights to a group, but whether, and if so how, this applies to language groups is at the centre of controversies about the protection of minorities and thus Indigenous languages, all of which are nowadays spoken in state territories. Does a shared language unite individuals to form a group for common interests and moral purposes and thus qualify it to bear rights? This is a question which concerns many signatories of the Charter for Regional or Minority Languages, Germany, for example. In a commentary on the constitutional law of the Federal Republic of Germany within the European Union we find the following statement which corresponds with similar pronouncements in other European legal contexts.

> In state constitutional law, the protection of minority languages belongs primarily in the larger context of minority protection. The protection of the language is an essential element of the protection of minorities and their cultural identity as a whole. For the importance

> of language as an identity-forming element cannot be underestimated, especially for groups with close cultural ties within a majority society. *It is not for nothing that discrimination against minorities, both in the present and in the past, often begins with the ban on using their native language* (emphasis added). In addition, there is a strengthening of the protection of individual fundamental rights in terms of collective law, since the use of language is a central instrument of the fundamentally protected free development of personality. The protection of minority languages therefore has in cultural constitutional law both an element of collective law and an element of individual law.[15]

The principal concern, it can be concluded from this historically grounded comment, is the prevention of discrimination which concerns both individual and collective law. However, there is no consensus in political philosophy as to how this can be realized. As mentioned above, there are broadly two positions that face each other. On one hand there is the view, supported, e.g., by Kymlicka (2007) and other multiculturalists, that in a democratic state discrimination can best be avoided by accepting minorities as they are and supporting them in their attempts to cultivate their identity; and on the other it is argued, e.g., by Barry (2001), that cultivating separate identities perpetuates isolation and stigmatization and can only undermine the equality that uniform national citizenship must guarantee to all individuals regardless of their cultural particularities. In this view, the marginalization of linguistic minorities in the modern state is inevitable.[16] In the best interest of socio-economic justice, cultural, including linguistic, distinctions must be played down or even ignored, argue the latter, while the former maintain that fairness demands the recognition of diversity which must be (made) compatible with equality, especially socio-economic equality and equal opportunity.

In the United States, the national language question and the socio-political treatment of minority languages are the subject of long-standing debates. A position that is inimical to linguistic minorities is represented by various movements, most prominently US English, as mentioned in Chapter 3, which want to make English the national language and bar all other languages from official discourse.[17] On the other hand, to promote political participation and increase voter turnout, several US states publish multilingual voting rights flyers, such as Massachusetts, in Arabic, Chinese, Haitian Creole, Portuguese, Spanish, and Vietnamese, in addition to English, though conspicuously not in an Indigenous language.[18]

All of these examples attest that avoiding discrimination of individuals and population groups in the spirit of human rights is today more widely accepted as a desirable policy goal than in former times, but there is no consensus on how to achieve it. The bipolar discussion about individual vs. group rights sketched above continues, which is testimony to a very complex reality of various, partly overlapping national and supranational legal norms, and languages variously designated as national, official, regional and minority languages, territorial languages—with historical roots in the country in question—and non-territorial languages that arrived in a (relatively recent) migratory context. Because these complexities meet different traditions and policy preferences in different countries, it is well-nigh impossible to draw general conclusions about how the imperative to protect minorities is being implemented and how it is helping to reverse or at least halt the decline of Indigenous languages.

Language recognition

One of the unresolved difficulties concerns language recognition, i.e., the demarcation of certain ways of speaking or signing as a language. If a language is to be introduced into the education system or to be taken into account in public administration and other contexts that might be conducive to language maintenance, its existence and differentiation from others must be demonstrated. Given that languages are perpetually changing, and language community affiliations potentially as well, this is a challenge both conceptually and in practice. Perhaps this is more evident outside European contexts, where the perception of language has been so strongly shaped by the national language ideology. Consider China.

The Republic of China (ROC), predecessor of the People's Republic of China (PRC) founded in 1949, recognized five ethnicities and their languages symbolically represented by the state's five-coloured flag: red, yellow, blue, white, and black for the 'Five Races Under One Union', the Han, the Manchus, the Mongols, the Hui (Uyghurs), and the Tibetans, respectively. Today, as the result of decades of ethnolinguistic research and in accordance with the PRC's 1982 constitution and the Regional Ethnic Autonomy Law of 1984, the Chinese government recognizes 55 such groups, in addition to the majority Han Chinese.[19] All 56 officially recognized ethnic groups and their languages nominally enjoy equal status and the Chinese government promotes learning both regional languages and Mandarin Chinese, but in practice Chinese and those minority languages that potentially pose a threat to the PCR's national integrity are privileged with regard to use and development (Zhou 2004: 90). Moreover, it is well known that the number of China's Indigenous languages is much higher, but many of them are unwritten and hence not easily distinguished and not (yet) recognized.

Or take India, undoubtedly the most linguistically diverse country in the world. The Indian Constitution recognizes 23 languages, a small fraction of the varieties in use throughout the country. The Linguistic Survey of India, which is regularly conducted in conjunction with the general census, estimated the number of languages and dialects spoken as 'mother tongues' at 19,569 in 2011, where mother tongue is understood as 'the language mainly spoken in the person's home in childhood'.[20] That this number is more than double the commonly quoted number of the world's languages shows that such numbers are in the eye of the beholder. The term 'mother tongue' seems to be especially fuzzy, but many studies have shown that other terms such as 'national language' can be just as vague, contested, and politically charged[21].

Because such indefiniteness is not exceptional but lies in the very nature of language, the 1996 Universal Declaration of Linguistic Rights proclaimed 'the equality of linguistic rights, without any non-pertinent distinctions between official/non-official/regional/local, majority/minority, or modern/archaic languages' and considered collective and individual aspects of these rights to be inseparable.[22]

The declaration does not use these terms because, though 'in certain cases they can facilitate the exercise of certain rights, these and other modifiers are frequently used to restrict the rights of language communities' (Article 5). The declaration's central raison d'être as explained in its preamble is to counter 'the age-old unifying tendency of the majority of States to reduce diversity and to foster attitudes opposed to cultural plurality and linguistic pluralism'.

This pluralism, according to the declaration (Section on Concepts, 4) comprises nomad peoples, immigrants, refugees, deported persons, and members of diasporas which are explicitly mentioned as examples of language groups to be considered by the declaration. This perspective on the position of minorities in multicultural and multilingual states is inherently universalist and hence at variance with ideas on ways of organizing linguistic diversity promoted by nation states. Since within the framework of this declaration collective and individual rights to use and cultivate a language are treated as inseparable, the legal question whether and under what conditions languages can form the basis of group rights remains unresolved.

Linguistic citizenship

The Universal Declaration of Linguistic Rights did not result in concrete legislation, but its content is still inspirational for those interested in developing policies to empower Indigenous language communities and other marginalized groups, and to advance the international discourse on reducing power asymmetries between language communities: a recent new concept which, like the declaration, renounces the categorization of languages, advocates an alternative to the linguistic human rights-based approach: 'linguistic citizenship' (Lim, Stroud, and Wee 2018). Proponents of this model argue that conceptualizing language-related state-society relations in terms of rights may inadvertently increase rather than decrease the potential for conflict between speakers of different languages/varieties. Instead, the notion of linguistic citizenship shall encourage speakers of all languages spoken on a territory to exercise agency and participation. Although it is embedded in institutionalized democratic structures, it goes beyond them where the privileging of one or a couple of languages on the part of the state is to the disadvantage of marginal groups 'whose voices are habitually silenced' (Stroud 2018: 4). This is clearly a counter design to the native speaker as a citizen of an essentially unilingual state, which in the best of cases takes precautions to tolerate local minorities.

The idea that citizenship should encompass all residents regardless of the language/variety they habitually speak was first developed in South Africa, a country with 11 official languages—Afrikaans, English, Xhosa, Zulu, Southern Sotho, Tswana, Northern Sotho, Tsonga, Venda, Swati, and Ndebele—and many more without official status in active use. It is an environment where the critique of essentializing languages and ethnicities is convincing. If South Africa's multilingualism has inspired the notion of multilingual citizens, it also seems suitable in other multilingual post-colonial contexts in Africa where many examples are found that diversity does not have to lead to disunity. Many African countries are at an earlier stage of nation building with a wide array of ethnolinguistic groups not all of which are clearly separated, and the question can be asked whether following European models of 'mother tongue', 'national language', and 'minority language' is the most productive language policy in such situations. It is by no means clear that prescriptions offered in legal and constitutional terms are the best strategy for maintaining and promoting peaceful co-existence. The idea of linguistic citizenship that ignores status differences between languages might offer a path forward that differs from European preconceptions that are based on a standardized written language model, clear divisions, and exclusive identities.

Open questions

Linguistic multitude and especially the position of Indigenous linguistic minorities in contemporary states can be viewed from a variety of different language policy perspectives. There is wide agreement that, but not how, they should be protected from decay. This is because in this particular field, as in others, policies cannot easily be abstracted from historically grown language regimes or sociocultural and economic policy concerns. Controversy in political philosophy also persists: the liberal position emphasizes non-interference on the part of the state and understands rights and universal values as pertaining to individuals only, whereas more community-oriented viewpoints allow for collective rights, such as the right of language choice by groups which implies obligations for the state.

How politically important is language today, and how important linguistic diversity? As pointed out previously, the United Nations General Assembly proclaimed the period between 2022 and 2032 as the International Decade of Indigenous Languages. Is this more than a romantic response to the uncertainties induced by the maelstroms of globalization? I will not pretend to know the answer, but this initiative will likely stimulate research on Indigenous languages, thereby helping policymakers and civil society representatives to develop strategies that benefit the communities in question and dispel negative attitudes from both majority societies as well as their members themselves. Language policy is contingent and ideologically embedded. Further evidence for this assertion can be found in the final chapter.

Further reading

Atlas of the World's Languages in Danger. UNESCO Digital Library. https://unesdoc.unesco.org/ark:/48223/pf0000187026

Council of Europe. 2004. *The European Charter for Regional and Minority Languages and the French Dilemma: Diversity v. unicity – Which Language for the Republic?* Strasbourg: Council of Europe.

Grin, François. 2005. Linguistic human rights as a source of policy guidelines: A critical assessment. *Journal of Sociolinguistics* 9: 448–460.

Kabel, Ahmed. 2023. From neoliberal to decolonial language rights and reparative linguistic justice. In T. Skutnabb-Kangas and R. Phillipson (eds.), *The Handbook of Linguistic Human Rights*. Oxford: Wiley Blackwell, 159–173.

Ricento, Thomas, Yael Peled, and Peter Ives (eds.) 2014. Language Policy and Political Theory. *Language Policy* 13, 4 (special issue).

11

Anti-discrimination policies

> Tagged: #gender-inclusive #expressions #gendersensible #language
>
> Notes on using non-discriminatory language
>
> If a person makes you aware that certain words or phrases are hurtful or perceived as discriminatory, take it seriously and avoid using these expressions.
>
> If you are told how a person self-identifies and wishes to be addressed, try to use their preferred name and pronouns.[1]

Many states have anti-discrimination laws designed to ensure that people are not excluded or otherwise discriminated against on the basis of race, colour, national origin, age, religion, disability, sex, gender identity, language, or other classifications. Over the past half century, the implications of such laws for language policy on the micro level have garnered much scholarly and societal attention. Language is our most important means of communication, and it isn't neutral, or perhaps better, it is hard, many would say impossible, to use it in a neutral way that depicts the world as it is, because we are born into and grow up in a certain time at a certain place. That has been known for a long time. Words and ways of speaking may reflect our state of knowledge, favour attitudes, values, and meanings which change with social developments. To what extent is it possible and desirable to influence the evolving relationship between language and society, and who should do this in a democratic state? As some examples will show, the division of labour and competence in this regard can be controversial because it is historically contingent and politically loaded.

Language Policy. Florian Coulmas, Oxford University Press. © Florian Coulmas (2025).
DOI: 10.1093/9780191976377.003.0011

Iel

In 2021, the word *iel* (plural *iels*), a merging of the French third person pronouns *il* (he) and *elle* (she), was declared the word of the year in francophone Switzerland.[2] Historically contingent? Well, no one interested in these matters would deny that this not only did not happen in 1921, but could not have happened then, when female suffrage was still fifty years off in Switzerland. In the same year the online edition of the esteemed French dictionary *Le Robert* for the first time included the new word[3]—and all hell broke loose.

Le Robert's decision sparked a public controversy in the media, in which, among many others, the highest guardian of linguistic decency then-French Minister of Education Jean-Michel Blanquer got involved. Taking a very clear position he stated that 'I obviously support @FJolivet36's protest vis-à-vis the #PetitRobert. Inclusive writing[4] is not the future of the French language.'[5] François Jolivet was a member of the French National Assembly where he represented the department of Indre for the party *La République En Marche!* He had written and published a lengthy letter to the Académie française accusing *Le Robert*'s authors of giving in to an activist agenda 'that has nothing to do with French'.

This debate is of interest for several reasons. First, even a word that has no lexical meaning but only a deictic function can become the object of heated arguments. 'Lexical meaning' and 'deictic function' are theoretical terms in linguistics that the man in the street—whoops: person!—isn't necessarily familiar with. Deictic terms have no fixed reference. *I* refers to me when I use it, but to you when you use it, and so with other situational terms with variable reference in relation to temporal (*today*), spatial (*here*), and social (*the Right Honourable*) contexts among others. Pronouns of first, second, and third person change their referent with use. In French, as well as in English and several other languages, first and second person pronouns are not marked for gender, while singular third person pronouns are gendered: *il* (m), *elle* (f). In other languages, Hebrew for example, second person pronouns singular and plural are also marked for gender: *you* is always either *you* (f) or *you* (m). And in other languages, Chinese for example, pronouns are typically gender neutral (cf. Mühlhäusler and Harré 1990 for more examples).

Where is the notebook? Don't you see it? It's on the table.
Où est *le* cahier? Vous ne *le* voyez pas? C'est sur la table.

In French, 'don't you see it?' becomes 'don't you see *him*?' because there are two grammatical genders in French and *cahier* 'notebook' happens to be masculine. Or consider German which has three grammatical genders, as for instance *die Gabel* (f) 'fork', *das Messer* (n, i.e., neuter) 'knife', *der Löffel* (m) 'spoon' (Table 16). It also has double gender nouns like *die See* 'the sea' and *der See* 'the lake'. Is there anything feminine about seas and forks, or masculine about lakes and spoons? Clearly not, which is to show that grammatical gender is a feature of some languages but not of others, that it has nothing to do with 'natural gender' (sex) and therefore gender shouldn't be an issue. But things get more complicated when people are addressed and talked about in social contexts and grammatical gender and natural gender interfere.

Table 16 Grammatical gender of cutlery in three languages

English	French	German
fork	fourche (f)	Gabel (f)
knife	couteau (m)	Messer (n)
spoon	cuiller (f)	Löffel (m)

German *Löffel* is masculine and therefore *der* 'he' in a relative clause, for example. Similarly, the French word *président*, too, is masculine and is therefore referred to in dependent clauses with masculine pronouns, i.e., *il* or *lui*. However, this is not just because of the structural peculiarities of the French language, but because presidents are thought of as male—no female president since the French Revolution—a perception that is reinforced by the grammatical gender of the words designating them; or so the argument for the promotion of non-sexist language usage goes. 'Social gender' is a term that has gained some currency among researchers who are trying to get a grip on the interaction between social and linguistic dynamics. It refers to the characteristics of women, men, girls, and boys that are socially constructed. Expressions in English, such as *male nurse* and *female nurse*, illustrate this. The former has a higher frequency of occurrence than the latter because the social gender of nurse is female. With *lady doctor* it is the reverse, the social gender of medics (in Western societies) being male.

Eliminating language use that is based on males as the tacit norm has been a demand of feminist sociolinguists and philosophers of language for the past half century (Mills 2008; Motschenbacher 2014). Generic masculine has been a target, i.e., terms such as *man* (as *man in the street*) and *he* used to cover both men and women ought to be avoided because they reduce women's importance in social life. Changing habitual language use patterns in order to increase the visibility of women is a policy objective that spread from anglophone contexts to other parts of the Western world and beyond. Feminine generics—using *she*, *her*, *hers* throughout instead of *he*, *him*, *his*—is one strategy of countering androcentric structures, but not a very successful one because this usage remains highly marked.

More effective was non-binary singular *they*, which spread quickly. Receiving ever more inquiries about its correct use, Miriam-Webster declared it its word of the year in 2019 telling their(!) readers that there was something surprising about this choice, namely that 'even a basic term, among the most common in the language—a personal pronoun—can rise to the top of our data'.[6] There were some comments about it, but nothing like the storm *iel* unleashed in the francophone tea cup. This raises two further questions regarding the 2021 debate about it. One, is getting worked up about words a French peculiarity? And two, what does the debate about *iel* reveal about the conceptualization of language?

The answer to the first question is: yes and no. Yes, because (im)proper language use, new words, fashionable formulations, etc. are always good for animated debates in France (Ager 1999), which suggests a pronounced social interest in language. In view of the prestigious position of the French Academy discussed above (p. 61) this is not surprising and reminds us that language policy is always embedded in cultural attitudes. No, because France/the francophone world is not alone. It is not difficult to find other examples of languages that are emotionally charged and rank highly in the esteem, appreciation, and attention of their speakers. Differing responses to the inclusion of a gender-neutral pronoun in highly regarded French and English dictionaries indicate culturally variable attitudes towards language policies and their implication at the micro level, which leads us to the second question.

Eventually the debate about *iel* can also be seen as implying an argument about the nature of language, how it evolves and how it relates to social reality. We can distinguish three positions. Nineteenth-century linguistic nationalism portrayed language as an organic being which in its evolution follows something like natural laws that cannot be tinkered with. Twentieth century structuralism saw language not as a natural phenomenon, but, as its most prominent representative Ferdinand de Saussure put it, following French sociologist Émile Durkheim[7], 'a social fact', a system of signs with fixed meanings and grammatical structures that evolve following system-internal dynamics. Finally, in a twenty-first century post-structuralist conceptualization the language system is socially constructed and amenable to reform much like other social conventions. According to this view, grammatical gender is a social construct that reflects societal structures and can be changed at will. In contrast, those taking offence to *iel* (or singular *they*, etc.) endorse language-inherent properties that must be respected, or at least use such a conception to support their arguments against arbitrary change. They may in fact have no clear conception of language at all but just a conservative agenda that change is corruption.

The French education minister Jean-Michel Blanquer quoted above apparently sides with those crediting language with inherent properties. Adding *iel* to the French lexicon is unacceptable because, that was Jolivet's argument, it 'has nothing to do with French'. It is possible, we must conclude, to distinguish what is from what is not, and cannot be, French, and Mr Jolivet knows the difference. This is a little ironic because French is the paradigm case of a normatively regulated language where what does and does not belong to it is not determined by its inherent nature but by externally set standards. It is on the basis of this very idea that advocates of gender neutrality argue that lexical innovation can be guided, new terms like *iel* can be deliberately invented, and alternative terms for derogatory words, such as *****, can be promoted.

French is one of the official languages of the United Nations, which has proved to be quite sensitive to questions of discrimination expressed through language use and therefore issues guidelines for inclusive language, also for French. It is, perhaps, because of the French government's critical position in this regard that the UN recommendations are phrased very cautiously as follows:

> Avoid stereotypes and discriminatory or negative expressions.
> Make gender visible where appropriate.
> Don't make gender visible if the context lends itself to it.[8]

Where making gender visible and the context lends itself to it is a matter of choice and subjective assessment, which eventually will be reflected in dictionaries and other reference works. *Le Robert*, which considers itself a descriptive rather than prescriptive record of French words, takes a position somewhere in between advocates and opponents of inclusive language and rejected the protest launched against its authors because the task of dictionaries is to record words in common use, including many that reflect new ideas or social trends. Their listing in the dictionary, obviously, says nothing about whether or not *Le Robert* supports these ideas.

Still, it can be asked what dictionaries can and should record. A difference between the French and English gender-neutral pronouns under discussion here is instructive in this regard. *Iel* sticks out since it is for everyone to see an artificially coined new word, whereas *they* is 'among the most common' words in English. *Iel* is about a new entry in the dictionary and changing conventions by means of a word which in its composition symbolizes what it is meant to accomplish, gender neutrality, which goes counter to the 'nature' of French. Singular *they*, on the other hand, is just a matter of extending the use of a well-known word that has been a dictionary entry and actually been used in singular meaning for a long time. ('Everyone should know, they can do it if they want to.') This may be one reason why it met with less resistance than *iel*. That gender-binary structures are much less deeply rooted in English than in French is another. This also holds for other languages which, as discussed above, are characterized by different ways of encoding gender and for which gender-neutral formulations are accordingly more difficult or impossible to develop (Motschbacher 2014). In some languages for which gender neutrality was sought, strategies for writing were developed that do not correspond to anything in speech, as, for instance the 'median-period' added to French masculine nouns and followed by the feminine ending as in *musicien·ne·s* for 'male musicians and female musicians' instead of the generic masculine. In German, an asterisk, the 'gender star', came to be used in a similar way: *Verbraucher*innen* which is shorter than *Verbraucher und Verbraucherinnen* 'male and female consumers'. In speech it has become represented by a glottal stop, that is, a minute pause in the pronunciation of the asterisked word.

Beyond gender

The feminist agenda of giving women more visibility pioneered attempts to tackle inequality in Western societies from the point of view of language use. It was later augmented by a more inclusive discourse about gender, sex, sexual orientation, and language, and then, more widely still, about representing disenfranchised groups generally, how to refer to them and giving them a voice in politics. Obviously, this isn't just about words, but about how language relates to and depicts society.

Although we may all on occasion use what others consider rude expressions without being aware of it, it is generally not hard to agree that offensive wording should be avoided. What should be done to enforce such a general principle and who should be tasked with its oversight are more delicate questions. A prime reason for this is that offensiveness is not a property of words but a matter of, shall we say, taste, perception, or mode? *Négritude*, for example, was an anti-colonial, anti-racist, and anti-Eurocentric intellectual movement that came up in Paris in the 1930s. If it were founded today, it wouldn't be called that, the

'N-word' having been tabooed.[9] Another example is Dutch *pinda*, which means 'peanut' but when used to refer to people with an East Indian background is a racist slur. With more than a quarter of the population originating from former colonies and other parts of the world, the Netherlands has long searched for appropriate terms for the various groups. In 1971, a government report introduced the term *allochtoon* for foreign-born population groups, and for some time, the distinction between *autochtoon* and *allochtoon* was accepted as descriptive and non-discriminatory. But by the mid-2010s the expiry date of these terms was approaching. In 2016 the House of Representatives in The Hague adopted a motion requesting the government to review the terms, because *allochtoon* had become increasingly perceived as stigmatizing (Leerkes and Dagevos 2016). A typical case of an innocuous term being compromised by use. Thus, much depends on context and speakers' intentions. Letting go of such formulation habits isn't difficult, nor is it to sensitize pupils at elementary school to avoid them. But beyond that, who should monitor what has been called 'verbal hygiene' (Cameron 1995)? Church? Government? Civil society? Pressure groups? Internet platforms?

The political correctness (PC) debate (Dunant 1994) that raged in the United States in the 1990s and has not completely abated to this day points in one direction; EU legislation in another. In the age of hate speech when the reach of offensive and inflammatory language is greater than ever, effective language policy seems more pressing than ever. PC advocates can be credited with foregrounding problems of discrimination relating to sexuality, gender, ethnicity, language, and race that have long been neglected, but the foundation of their authority to correct others' ways of speaking is doubtful. Is this a case of a minority gifted with superior knowledge and morality to redeem the majority from their ignorance? And should corrective actions be directed at the habits of speakers or the language they speak, for instance replacing the generic masculine with the generic feminine, or a binary world by a more inclusive one, symbolized by *they/iel*, etc.? If, as many PC supporters maintain, a language is a social construct and a common good of the language community, where is the power and authority to set it right? Should policing the language be the language policy answer to this question?

A positive answer would inevitably highlight another problem, i.e., that of freedom of expression and who should protect it. Is it legitimate to alter the language in order to effect social change and thereby curtail free speech? Or, better: curtail freedom of expression in a different way than it is curtailed anyway (in a civilized society)? If so, how close does this bring us to Newspeak, on the one hand, and to a surveillance state, on the other, assuming that the state is in charge? And if it's not the state, then is it a better alternative to rely on internet tycoons to accomplish the task? We must be clear that this is not a hypothetical question, but a new challenge for language policy engendered by technological change and the shift in the political typography of public expression it brought with it. This is one of the reasons why the European Union decided to make linguistic abuse an offence, as detailed in the Council Framework Decision 2008/913/JHA of 28 November 2008 on combating certain forms and expressions of racism and xenophobia by means of criminal law. Article 1 demonstrates what this is about.

Article 1

Offences concerning racism and xenophobia

1. Each Member State shall take the measures necessary to ensure that the following intentional conduct is punishable:
   (a) publicly inciting to violence or hatred directed against a group of persons or a member of such a group defined by reference to race, colour, religion, descent or national or ethnic origin;
   (b) the commission of an act referred to in point (a) by public dissemination or distribution of tracts, pictures or other material;
   (c) publicly condoning, denying or grossly trivialising crimes of genocide, crimes against humanity and war crimes as defined in Articles 6, 7 and 8 of the Statute of the International Criminal Court, directed against a group of persons or a member of such a group defined by reference to race, colour, religion, descent or national or ethnic origin when the conduct is carried out in

a manner likely to incite to violence or hatred against such a group or a member of such a group;

(d) publicly condoning, denying or grossly trivialising the crimes defined in Article 6 of the Charter of the International Military Tribunal appended to the London Agreement of 8 August 1945, directed against a group of persons or a member of such a group defined by reference to race, colour, religion, descent or national or ethnic origin when the conduct is carried out in a manner likely to incite to violence or hatred against such a group or a member of such a group.[10]

Notice that this law does not contain any specific terms. This is not because, like all EU laws, it is formulated and published in the 24 official languages of the Union, but because laws should apply for as long as possible and independently of changing stylistic habits of the kind illustrated by the above-mentioned example of Dutch *allochtoon*. Language is always a collective product and meaning, therefore, cannot be finally fixed, as the ideological load of words keeps changing. The law is nevertheless specific regarding expressions of racism and xenophobia directed against 'a group of persons or a member of such a group defined by reference to race, colour, religion, descent or national or ethnic origin'. Of course, this selection of categories also reflects attitudes and values of the era in which the law was passed. Expressions that a court of law decides fall into one of these categories are not protected in the European Union by the principle of freedom of expression.

A question that comes up here is whether the policy cycle model (see p. 8) could be applied to the EU Council Framework Decision 2008/913/JHA. Given the detailed instructions of Article 1, this should be possible, but ever-changing standards of proper conduct, including in relation to racism and xenophobia, make it difficult. In any case, policy implementation based on the Council Framework Decision functioning as policy formulation will be necessary.

We can see here a clash of two principles, both of paramount importance in liberal democracies. Prioritizing the one or the other is a political decision, likely to generate debate in each individual case, as political questions do. If this were not the case, there would be no need to write books about language policy because language would not be a political issue. Still, it is sometimes surprising how heated these debates become, giving the impression that language is just the stage on which to pursue further goals. For activists who see language reform as a lever for creating a better world this is probably so. Their arguments have often been countered by pointing out that turning *chairmen* into *chairpersons* or *chair* and *Clothes make the man* into *Clothes make the woman/person/human being* does little to change gender relations in 'real' terms, for instance regarding wage gaps and job opportunities. This may be so, but then, what's wrong with more inclusive language and changing or avoiding formulations that others find annoying?! That this 'has nothing to do with' language X is not a convincing argument because lexical and other innovations are ultimately decided on in communication by the language community. The actual effects of attempted and implemented language reforms are the subject of empirical research on how the community deals with them.

Effects and effectiveness

Thanks to new recording and data archiving technologies, statistics about stylistic preferences and frequencies of occurrence of words, at least in writing, are today readily available. Figure 4, for instance, shows

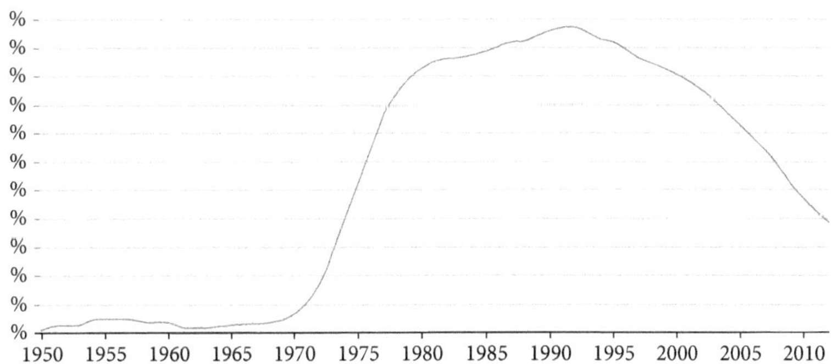

Figure 4 Frequency of occurrence of "chairperson" in a corpus of written British English, as measured by Google Ngram Viewer

that the frequency of occurrence of *chairperson* increased quite suddenly from the 1970s and peaked in 1992, paralleling the initial and most active decades of anti-sexist language politics. Then the curve flattened out and the *chairperson* boom was over for reasons we can speculate about, possibly because *chairman*, *chairwoman*, and *chairperson* were all supplanted by *chair*. Be this as it may, what conclusions can be drawn from this kind of observation is a much more intricate question. What does the increased frequency of the word correspond to in society? Even more difficult: if changes in gender relations over the same period of time—in the labour market, in politics, in the distribution of wealth—are observed, can causal connections be established? Did changing choice of expressions have any effect at all? Because of the multifarious relations between social and linguistic hierarchies—hierarchical relations between groups and members of linguistic communities, between ways of speaking and between languages—because of the never-ending activities of creating a common language for society, and because of the many conflicts that language generates and helps to resolve, this is extremely difficult to decide.

These complexities defy explanations in terms of unidimensional models of cause and effect. That gender-neutral formulations, in English and in other languages, have in themselves changed the world to the better, few would contend, but that does not mean that linguistic change has no effect at all and that attempts to bring them about are moot. Just by directing attention to the fact that there are alternatives to the m/f divide or categorizing people as either *autochtoon* or *allochtoon* may contribute in however indirect ways to transforming the political and moral landscape, and with it society.

Balancing the relative effects on language and usage of legislation on the one hand and advocacy activism on the other is equally difficult. In the academic field of language policy there is a conspicuous lack of data that can confirm the effectiveness of both approaches. Monitoring the institutionalized language policies on the macro level, for example government decisions concerning the use or discontinuation of language X for official purposes, is not so difficult, but effectiveness checks for micro level policies are more problematic, since causal relationships are hard to establish and relevant data involve the entire language community.

Instead of looking for cause and effect, it is more productive to analyse changes of language use in line with either the demands of activists or anti-discrimination legislation as part of larger transformations of recent decades in many post-industrial societies towards a wider acceptance of more diverse sexual orientations than a strictly binary order, multi-ethnic populations, multilingualism, and multiculturalism. Language policy is not a one-way street. At issue is not only how effective it is to bring about social change, but also how it responds to social change.

Rather than asking what a certain language policy has accomplished, we will then ask how such a policy fits into a wider agenda to promote understanding, mutual respect, and intercultural dialogue. In this agenda language plays a central role, as the general faculty that enables us to communicate and cooperate, as a means for executing innumerable specific tasks, as inexhaustible treasury of signs to represent the changing world in ever new ways, as the commons of group formation and instrument and symbol of power to exclude others. At a time when South-North migration is a global challenge and the tendency to make everything public is subjecting almost all communication to commercial and government surveillance, the great proliferation of literature on language policy over the past half century indicates, I believe, that we have become more aware of the importance of this instrument and its political dimensions. Given the progressive developments just mentioned, language policy will continue to command our attention.

Further reading

Alim, H. Samy, John R. Rickford, and Arnetha F. Ball (eds.) 2016. *Raciolinguistics. How Language Shapes our Ideas About Race.* New York: Oxford University Press.

Cameron, Deborah. 1998. *The Feminist Critique of Language, second edition.* London and New York: Routledge.

Dunant, Sarah (ed.) 1994. *The War of the Words. The Political Correctness Debate.* London: Virago Press.

Petričević, Vanja. 2015. *Compliance Patterns with European Union Anti-Discrimination Legislation.* London: Palgrave Macmillan.

Notes

Chapter 1

1. https://theconversation.com/long-before-shots-were-fired-a-linguistic-power-struggle-was-playing-out-in-ukraine-178247
2. Luke Harding, The Guardian 6 March 2023 https://www.theguardian.com/world/2023/mar/06/russia-ukrainians-embrace-language-war
3. The Language of Russia's War on Ukraine. Alexander J. Motyl, *Foreign Policy*, 13 March 2022. https://foreignpolicy.com/2022/03/13/putin-ukraine-russia-war-language-shibboleth-palyanitsya/

Chapter 2

1. Cf., for example, *Language Testing International*. https://www.languagetesting.com/proficiency-scales.
2. Cf. the *UNESCO Atlas of the World's Languages in Danger*, first published in 1996. https://unesdoc.unesco.org/ark:/48223/pf0000187026.
3. Hult and Cassels Johnson (2015) offer an overview of the available research methods in language policy.

Chapter 3

1. University https://slavic.fas.harvard.edu/bcs
2. Weber, Max. 1968 [1921]. *Economy and Society. An Outline of Interpretive Sociology*. Berkeley.: University of California Press, pp. 395; 922.
3. Cf. official English translation of Belgian Constitution at: https://www.dekamer.be/kvvcr/pdf_sections/publications/constitution/GrondwetUK.pdf
4. Information about the Taalunie in English can be found here: https://taalunie.org/informatie/112/taalunie-union-for-the-dutch-language
5. https://laws-lois.justice.gc.ca/eng/acts/o-3.01/
6. The official text of Bill C-13: https://www.parl.ca/DocumentViewer/en/44-1/bill/C-13/first-reading
7. Pierre Elliott Trudeau, in a statement upon introducing the Official Languages Bill, 17 October 1968. https://www.edu.gov.mb.ca/k12/cur/socstud/foundation_gr6/blms/6-3-2g.pdf
8. https://www.justice.gc.ca/eng/csj-sjc/rfc-dlc/ccrf-ccdl/rfcp-cdlp.html#s6
9. https://www.canada.ca/en/canadian-heritage/services/funding/aboriginal-peoples/languages.html
10. https://montrealgazette.com/news/local-news/breaking-down-the-key-points-of-bill-96
11. Cf. James Crawford. *Language Legislation in the U.S.A.* http://www.languagepolicy.net/archives/langleg.htm

12. New York State Education Department. 2020. Bilingual Education Toolkit. https://www.nysed.gov/sites/default/files/programs/bilingual-ed/brief-1_policy-and-regulation-final-a.pdf
13. Cf. Fact Sheet: Building a New Era of Nation-to-Nation Engagement. https://www.whitehouse.gov/briefing-room/statements-releases/2021/11/15/fact-sheet-building-a-new-era-of-nation-to-nation-engagement/
14. The website of the Parliament of the Federation of Bosnia and Herzegovina appears in Bosanski, Hrvatski, Srpski, that is, Bosnian, Croatian, and Serbian: https://parlamentfbih.gov.ba/v2/bs/index.php
15. A streaming of Jinnah's speech of 21 March, 1948 in Dhaka is accessible here: https://soundcloud.com/farazc21/muhammad-ali-jinnah-speech-at
16. UN International Mother Language Day: https://www.un.org/en/observances/mother-language-day
17. The languages listed in the Eighth Schedule are: Assamese, Bengali, Gujarati, Hindi, Kannada, Kashmiri, Konkani, Malayalam, Manipuri, Marathi, Nepali, Oriya, Punjabi, Sanskrit, Sindhi, Tamil, Telugu, Urdu, Bodo, Santhali, Maithili, and Dogri. https://www.mha.gov.in/sites/default/files/EighthSchedule_19052017.pdf

Chapter 4

1. For more details on Alisjahbana's work cf. Alisjahbana (1976), Coulmas (2016,Chapter 19).
2. Today still active as The Agency for Language Development and Cultivation in the Ministry of Education, Culture, Research, and Technology. https://kbi.kemdikbud.go.id/profil_eng.php
3. 'Asia for Asians' was the slogan Japan used to promote its expansion in the Asia Pacific.
4. Quoted from Grillo (1989: 190).
5. *Dictionnaire de l'Académie française*, Préface de la première édition (1694). https://www.academie-francaise.fr/le-dictionnaire-les-neuf-prefaces/preface-de-la-premiere-edition-1694
6. Quoted from Volker Harm. 2014. Das Grimmsche Wörterbuch, Stationen seiner Geschichte. *IDS Sprachreport* 1. https://ids-pub.bsz-bw.de/frontdoor/deliver/index/docId/3574/file/Harm_Grimmsche_Woerterbuch_2014_1.pdf

Chapter 5

1. https://www.reuters.com/world/europe/melonis-party-looks-shield-italian-language-foreign-contamination-2023-03-31/
2. https://roma.corriere.it/notizie/politica/23_aprile_02/rampelli-fdi-vicepresidente-della-camera-tutelare-l-italiano-non-e-autarchia-mangiare-un-croissant-si-si-puo-72ed0fc2-d0bd-11ed-8952-10f6bf0a23fa.shtml
3. Statistics Canada, https://www12.statcan.gc.ca/census-recensement/2021/ref/dict/az/definition-eng.cfm?ID=pop095
4. Cf. Bokhorst-Heng (1999: 242) about 'mother-tongue' in Singapore's *Speak Mandarin-Campaign.*
5. Croatian 6 m, Estonian 1 m, Finnish 5.8 m, Irish 1.9 m, Latvian 1.2 m, Lithuanian 2.8 m, Maltese 0.53 m, Slovenian 2.5 m. These are rough estimates, but these languages have fewer speakers than Catalan. Official status in the EU has never depended on speech community size. See https://european-union.europa.eu/principles-countries-history/languages_en
6. Cf. Pan South African Language Board at https://www.pansalb.org

7. http://www.academyofathens.gr/en/foundation/objectives
8. The Name *Kamal Atatürk* (*kamal* meaning 'strong') was bestowed on Mustafa Kemal as a matter of language policy on 24 November 1934 by a law that regulated family and first names.
9. Cf. The Turkish Language Association at https://tdk.gov.tr/
10. Various sources including Universal Translation Service https://www.universal-translation-services.com/english-speaking-countries-in-africa/, Frenchside https://frenchside.co.za/list-of-french-speaking-countries-in-africa/, Translators without Borders. Language data for Mozambique. https://translatorswithoutborders.org/language-data-for-mozambique
11. Figures are estimates based on various sources, such as World Atlas https://www.worldatlas.com/articles/what-languages-are-spoken-in-gabon.html and Translators without Borders https://translatorswithoutborders.org/
12. Translators without Borders. Language data for Mozambique. https://translatorswithoutborders.org/language-data-for-mozambique
13. Cf., for example, UNESCO. 2022. Why mother language-based education is essential. https://www.unesco.org/en/articles/why-mother-language-based-education-essential

Chapter 6

1. https://www.korean.go.kr/front_eng/roman/roman_01.do
2. https://www.britishcouncil.org/about-us/how-we-work
3. http://www.moe.gov.cn/s78/A19/
4. The motto of the Central Hindi Directorate is a verse from the *Rig Veda* in Sanskrit. Another translation, as Giridhar Rao of Azim Premji University informs me, is 'I am the Queen, the gatherer-up of treasures.'
5. http://www.academyofathens.gr/en
6. https://taalunie.org/over-de-taalunie-/wie-wij-zijn
7. Lia Rumantscha: https://www.liarumantscha.ch/rm
8. https://www.academie-francaise.fr/linstitution/les-missions
9. Rohsenow (2004: 24).
10. http://www.gov.cn/ziliao/flfg/2005-08/31/content_27920.htm
11. Cf. Li Yuming, Li Wei (2014) for a detailed documentation of recent and current legal and practical implementation of the standard spoken and written Chinese language.
12. http://www.gov.cn/ziliao/flfg/2005-08/31/content_27920.htm
13. For more details see Ministry of Justice of the Republic of Kazakhstan, Institute of legislation and Legal Information at: https://adilet.zan.kz/eng/docs/Z970000151_
14. Cf., for instance, *Oxford Languages, Word of the year* at: https://languages.oup.com/word-of-the-year/
15. https://www.vatican.va/content/benedict-xvi/en/motu_proprio/documents/hf_ben-xvi_motu-proprio_20121110_latina-lingua.html
16. Your visit to the official website of Pope Francis. https://www.vatican.va/content/vatican/en.html
17. For a review of how the Vatican is engaging with social media, see Rudolph Gehrig 2023. *The Digital Pope.* https://www.ewtnvatican.com/articles/digital pope-how-pope-francis-is-using-social-media-to-evangelize-874
18. Central Hindi Directorate, Programmes and Guidelines, http://chd.mhrd.gov.in/sites/default/files/programmes-and-guidelines-edition-2018compressed.pdf, p. 81.
19. The Eighth Schedule of the Indian Constitution lists the following languages: Assamese, Bengali, Bodo, Dogri, Gujarati, Hindi, Kannada, Kashmiri.
20. Ibid, p. 83.
21. Gandhi 1965: 65.

22. The Wire, 29 October 2022, https://thewire.in/video/official-language-committee-hindi-ptr-finance-miniter
23. The Guardian, 22 October 2022, https://www.theguardian.com/world/2022/oct/22/modi-employs-new-tool-in-indias-war-against-the-english-language-hindi-medical-degrees?CMP=Share_iOSApp_Other
24. See UNESCO 2005.
25. Cf. Coulmas (1989) for Japanese and Goh (2017) for Chinese.
26. The Chinese government discretely alludes to this on its International Education Exchange Information Platform: 'Benefiting from the UK, France, Germany and Spain's experience in promoting their national languages, China began its own exploration through establishing non-profit public institutions which aim to promote Chinese language and culture in foreign countries in 2004.' http://www.ieeip.cn/bbx/1071727-1123792.html?id=27381&newsid=715399

Chapter 7

1. https://www.ndtv.com/india-news/pm-narendra-modi-addresses-un-in-hindi-vajpayee-style-671752
2. https://www.un.org/en/our-work/official-languages
3. *About the Universal Declaration of Human Rights Translation Project.* https://www.ohchr.org/en/human-rights/universal-declaration/universal-declaration-human-rights/about-universal-declaration-human-rights-translation-project
4. United Nations. Official Languages. https://www.un.org/en/our-work/official-languages
5. Cf. For a comprehensive, if not always coherent, overview of the literature on linguistic human rights see Skutnabb-Kangas and Phillipson (2023).
6. Ricento (2012) offers a more detailed account of 'Global' English as a product of imperialism, vehicle of economic mobility, and instrument of justice.
7. WHO. Responding to Covid-19. Real-time training in national languages. https://openwho.org/channels/covid-19-national-languages
8. Cf., for example, Barbara Trudell. 2016. The impact of language policy and practice on children's learning. Evidence from Eastern and Southern Africa. UNICEF, https://www.unicef.org/esa/sites/unicef.org.esa/files/2018-09/UNICEF-2016-Language-and-Learning-Executive-Summary.pdf
9. Lozinskiy (2020, p. iv).
10. Lozinskiy (2020, p. iii).
11. European Commission, https://education.ec.europa.eu/focus-topics/improving-quality/multilingualism/about-multilingualism-policy
12. Centre de traduction des organs de l'Union Européenne: https://cdt.europa.eu/fr/contact-us. The centre presents itself, as one should expect, in the 24 official languages of the EU from Бългapcки (Bulgarian) to Svenska (Swedish).
13. https://eur-lex.europa.eu/legal-content/en/TXT/?uri=CELEX:12012E/TXT
14. The commission's use of languages (last updated: 11 July 2022). https://ec.europa.eu/info/about-european-commission/service-standards-and-principles/commissions-use-languages_en
15. European Parliament. 2019. Code of Conduct on Multilingualism, Article 1. https://www.europarl.europa.eu/about-parliament/files/organisation-and-rules/multilingualism/code-of-conduct_en.pdf
16. Rules of Procedure of the European Parliament, Chapter 3, Rule 167: https://www.europarl.europa.eu/doceo/document/lastrules/RULE-167_EN.html?redirect
17. The centre's key achievements in 2020: https://cdt.europa.eu/en/search/node?keys=number+of+pages+translated

18. https://ec.europa.eu/info/news/irish-now-same-level-other-official-eu-languages-2022-jan-03_en

Chapter 8

1. Keynes, John Maynard. 1980. The Collected Writings, Volume XXV: Activities, 1940–1944: Shaping the Post-war World. Basingstoke: The Clearing Union.
2. Kindleberger, Charles P. 1967. https://ies.princeton.edu/pdf/E61.pdf
3. Dhir, Krishna S. 2019.
4. https://www.imf.org/en/News/Articles/2015/09/28/04/53/sonew120115a
5. The European Commission states: 'Our globalised interconnected reality demands ever-smarter automatic translation tools.' It therefore invests massively in their development. Cf. https://cordis.europa.eu/article/id/441963-pushing-the-boundaries-of-automatic-translation
6. Bourdieu, Pierre. 1993. Sociology in Question. London: Sage, p. 80.
7. English UK. https://www.englishuk.com/facts-figures#value
8. Cf., for instance, British Council. 2013. The English Effect. https://www.britishcouncil.org/sites/default/files/english-effect-report-v2.pdf
9. Adam Smith, the father of economics as a scholarly discipline, had a keen interest in language which, on closer view, is related to his concern with understanding the development of human institutions. Cf. Considerations concerning the first formation of languages, first published as an appendix of Smith's *Theory of Moral Sentiments*, 1767.
10. Cf. Minority Monitor: https://minoritymonitor.eu/case/ESTONIA-THE-FORCED-ASSIMILATION-OF-THE-RUSSIAN-MINORITY-IS-NOW-CERTAIN
11. Breton, Roland J.-L. 2000. Can English be dethroned? The UNESCO Courier, 17-36. https://unesdoc.unesco.org/ark:/48223/pf0000119482
12. In recent years, economic language ranking has become a trend. Some examples: Alexika, 2018: Top Business Languages of the World for Exporters in the Global Marketplace. https://alexika.com/blog/2018/11/29/top-business-languages-of-the-world; Visual Capitalist, 2020: Ranked: The 100 Most Spoken Languages Around the World. https://www.visualcapitalist.com/100-most-spoken-languages/; The Local, 2021: The world's most powerful languages. https://www.thelocal.com/20211220/worlds-most-powerful-languages-which-will-you-learn-2022-escp-tlccu/; acolad, 2023: Going global: Top 10 languages for international business growth. https://www.acolad.com/en/services/consulting/most-demand-languages.html; University of the People, 2021: Companies are all global, and the demand for multilingual applicants is high. https://www.uopeople.edu/blog/most-important-languages-to-learn/; Resurchify, 2023: Language Value-Impact Score, Overall Ranking. https://www.resurchify.com/impact/details/21101028383
13. GDP by Country. Worldometer. https://www.worldometers.info/gdp/gdp-by-country/
14. GDP per Capita, https://www.worldometers.info/gdp/gdp-per-capita/
15. List of Countries by Literacy Rate. https://www.worldatlas.com/articles/the-highest literacy-rates-in-the-world.html
16. Lane, James. 2021. The ten most widely spoken languages in the world. Babble Magazine. https://www.babbel.com/en/magazine/the-10-most-spoken-languages-in-the-world
17. Duggan, Bill. 2021. Diversity is the 2021 Marketing Word of the Year. ANA Marketing Maestros, 7 December. https://www.ana.net/blogs/show/id/mm-blog-2021-12-diversity-word-of-the-year
18. UNESCO. 2022. Why mother-language-based education is essential. https://www.unesco.org/en/articles/why-mother-language-based-education-essential
19. Chan, Kai. 2016. These are the most powerful languages in the world. World Economic Forum. https://www.weforum.org/agenda/2016/12/these-are-the-most-powerful-languages-in-the-world/

20. Council of Europe Language Policy Portal. https://www.coe.int/en/web/language-policy/home#
21. Cf. European Parliament. 2020. Factsheets on the European Union—Language Policy. https://www.europarl.europa.eu/ftu/pdf/en/FTU_3.6.6.pdf
22. https://www.europarl.europa.eu/RegData/etudes/STUD/2016/573460/IPOL_STU(2016)573460_EN.pdf

Chapter 9

1. Gérald Darmanin wants to make residence permits conditional on mastery of a minimum level of French. Interior Minister Gérald Darmanin would like to make the issue of residence permits for foreign nationals conditional on their mastery of the French language. The government is going to propose to make issuing multi-annual residence permits (CSP) conditional on the mastery of a minimum level of French in order to promote integration, Interior Minister Gérald Darmanin announced on Tuesday, 12 July. Alexandre Chauveau, *Europe 1*, 13 July 2022. https://www.europe1.fr/politique/gerald-darmanin-veut-conditionner-la-carte-de-sejour-a-la-maitrise-dun-niveau-minimal-de-francais-4123041
2. Sources: https://www.statista.com/statistics/466078/number-citizenship-acquisitions-france/; Statistisches Bundesamt: https://www.destatis.de/DE/Presse/Pressemitteilungen/2022/06/PD22_237_125.html; https://www.statista.com/statistics/779378/acquisition-of-italian-citizenship-by-non-eu-citizens-italy/; Centraal Bureau voor Statistiek: https://www.cbs.nl/nl-nl/nieuws/2021/38/aantal-naturalisaties-in-2020-verdubbeld; Home Office: https://www.gov.uk/government/statistics/immigration-statistics-year-ending-december-2021/how-many-people-continue-their-stay-in-the-uk-or-apply-to-stay-permanently
3. Sometime around mid-November 2022. UN News, 15 November 2022: https://news.un.org/en/story/2022/11/1130632
4. For a brief overview see: Habermas, Jürgen. 1974. The Public Sphere: An Encyclopedia Article (1964). *New German Critique*, no. 3, 49–55. JSTOR, https://doi.org/10.2307/487737.
5. Cf., for example, Castles and Davidson. 2000; Shohamy and McNamara. 2009; Council of Europe. 2013; Bruzos, Erdocia, and Khan. 2018; and Shohamy. 2023, who puts particular emphasis on ethical issues and developing awareness of misuses of language tests for political purposes.
6. EU Blue Card Network: https://www.apply.eu/passport/
7. Cf. Third-country nationals' integration in the European Union: https://www.oecd-ilibrary.org/docserver/9789264307216-12-en.pdf?expires=1670931910&id=id&accname=guest&checksum=F48DC84EE92F4C09F08C11A3526479B9
8. Cf., for example, Yao, Wallace. 2021. Council of Europe Language Policy Portal at https://www.coe.int/en/web/language-policy
9. Ivy Kaplan (2018). How smartphones and social media have revolutionized refugee migration. https://www.unhcr.org/blogs/smartphones-revolutionized-refugee-migration/
10. https://commission.europa.eu/aid-development-cooperation-fundamental-rights/your-rights-eu/know-your-rights/citizens-rights/right-vote-and-stand-candidate-municipal-elections_en
11. Migration statistics are notoriously difficult because of variable categorizations. This estimate is from the UN's World Migration Report 2022. https://worldmigrationreport.iom.int/wmr-2022-interactive/
12. Various sources: https://www.macrotrends.net/cities/20142/antwerpen/population; https://www.bielefeld.de/sites/default/files/datei/2023/Bevoelkerung_31.12.2022.pdf; https://www.statista.com/statistics/862755/total-population-of-eindhoven/; https://ugeo.urbistat.com/AdminStat/de/at/demografia/dati-sintesi/stadt-linz/401/3; https://

ugeo.urbistat.com/AdminStat/en/it/demografia/stranieri/prato/100/3; https://www.ine.es/en/wel/faq_en.htm#3
13. For the concept of family language policy cf. Caldas (2012), and for a case study, Wąsikiewicz-Firlej, Daly (2023).

Chapter 10

1. https://www.coe.int/en/web/european-charter-regional-or-minority-languages. For a discussion of how the European Charter for Regional and Minority Languages relates to other instruments of the Council of Europe for the protection of minority languages cf. de Groot (2019).
2. International Covenant on Civil and Political Rights, Article II, 1. https://www.ohchr.org/en/instruments-mechanisms/instruments/international-covenant-civil-and-political-rights
3. For instance, Max Weber commented on scholars writing books about small languages as follows. 'In the 19th century the Romantic ideologists and their epigoni awakened numerous declining language groups of 'interesting' peoples to the purposive cultivation of their languages. German secondary and university teachers helped save small Slavic language groups, about whom they felt the intellectual need to write books' (Weber 1968: 3450). Weber clearly did not feel such a need.
4. Cf., for example, early milestones such as Dorian (1989) and Robins and Uhlenbeck (1991), and more recent and comprehensive Rehg and Campbell (2018).
5. For example, *The Endangered Languages Project.* https://www.endangeredlanguages.com/about/
6. Universal Declaration of Linguistic Rights, p. 13. https://culturalrights.net/descargas/drets_culturals389.pdf
7. Atlas of the World's Languages in Danger. https://unesdoc.unesco.org/arc:/48223/pf0000104267
8. Cf. Federally Recognized Indian Tribes and Resources for Native Americans. https://www.usa.gov/tribes
9. https://www.unesco.org/en/decades/Indigenous-languages
10. https://web.archive.org/web/20130212043919/http://www2.ohchr.org:80/english/law/ccpr.htm
11. https://oikeusministerio.fi/en/linguistic-rights
12. European Charter for Regional or Minority Languages (European Treaty Series No. 148). https://rm.coe.int/1680695175
13. European Commission 2021. Statistics on Migration to Europe. https://commission.europa.eu/strategy-and-policy/priorities-2019-2024/promoting-our-european-way-life/statistics-migration-europe_en
14. Ministry of Justice, Finland. *Linguistic Rights.* https://oikeusministerio.fi/en/linguistic-rights
15. Stern, Klaus, Helge Sodan, Markus Möstl (eds.). 2022 (second edition.). *Das Staatsrecht der Bundesrepublik Deutschland im europäischen Staatenverbund Gesamtwerk.* Munich: C.H. Beck, (Randnummer (paragraph) 68).
16. This debate is most apparent in Western, especially Anglo-American political theory, as May (2023) explains in a useful overview.
17. Cf. US English: https://www.usenglish.org/
18. https://www.mass.gov/info-details/multilingual-voting-rights-flyers
19. Cf. Hongkai Sun, Florian Coulmas (eds.)1992. News from China: Minority Languages in Perspective. *International Journal of the Sociology of Language* 97.
20. https://censusindia.gov.in/census.website/node/174
21. For discussion and some specific examples, cf. Maxwell (2003), Makoni, Pennycook (2007).

22. https://www.barcelona.cat/bcnmetropolis/2007-2017/en/dossier/la-declaracio-universal-de-drets-linguistics-vint-anys-despres/

Chapter 11

1. Goethe Universität Frankfurt am Main, studiumdigitale. https://lehre-virtuell.uni-frankfurt.de/knowhow/gender-inclusive-language-guidelines/
2. https://www.rsi.ch/news/svizzera/La-parola-italiana-dellanno-%C3%A8-penuria-15823642.html
3. https://dictionnaire.lerobert.com/definition/iel
4. Discussions about gender-neutral and inclusive writing had been going on for some time. In 2017, then prime minister Edouard Philippe had banned the use of gender-neutral French in government documents.
5. Je soutiens évidemment la protestation de @FJolivet36 vis-à-vis du #PetitRobert L'écriture inclusive n'est pas l'avenir de la langue française. https://twitter.com/jmblanquer/status/1460644816677744640?lang=en
6. https://www.merriam-webster.com/words-at-play/woty2019-top-looked-up-words-they
7. Cf. *Les règles de la méthode sociologique*, 1894. https://philosophie.universite.tours/documents/1894_Emile_Durkheim.pdf
8. See the UN https://www.un.org/fr/gender-inclusive-language/guidelines.shtml
9. The French word *nègre* is derived from Spanish *negro* and was adapted in the seventeenth century to English variously spelt as *neger*, *niger*, and *nigger*. Because of its association with the transatlantic slave trade it gradually fell out of use as offensive in the second half of the twentieth century (Rahman 2012).
10. https://eur-lex.europa.eu/legal-content/EN/TXT/?uri=celex%3A32008F0913

References

Ager, Dennis. 1999. *Identity, Insecurity and Image. France and Language.* Clevedon: Multilingual Matters.

Alim, H. Samy, John R. Rickford, and Arnetha F. Ball (eds.) 2016. *Raciolinguistics. How Language Shapes Our Ideas About Race.* New York: Oxford University Press.

Alisjahbana, S. Takdir. 1976. *Language Planning for Modernization: The Case of Indonesia and Malaysia.* The Hague: Mouton.

Alisjahbana, S. Takdir. 1984. The concept of language standardisation and its application to the Indonesian language. In Florian Coulmas (ed.) *Linguistic Minorities and Literacy: Language Policy Issues in Developing Countries.* Berlin, Boston: De Gruyter Mouton: 77–98. https://doi.org/10.1515/9783110865301.77

Anderson, Benedict. 1991. *Imagined Communities: Reflections on the Origin and Spread of Nationalism.* Revised edition. London: Verso.

Anwary, Afroza. 2011. Frame alignment and the dynamics of the national language movement of East Pakistan. *Journal of Asian History* 45: 163–191.

Aristotle. 1964. *Politics & Poetics.* Translated by Benjamin Jowett and S.H. Butcher, 1964. New York: Heritage Press.

UNESCO 2010. Atlas of the World's Languages in Danger. UNESCO Digital Library. https://unesdoc.unesco.org/ark:/48223/pf0000187026

Austin Peter K., Julia Sallabank (eds.) 2011. *The Cambridge Handbook of Endangered Languages.* Cambridge: Cambridge University Press.

Barry, Brian. 2001. *Culture and Equality: An Egalitarian Critique of Multiculturalism.* Cambridge, MA: Harvard University Press.

Bennis, Hans and Corrien Blom. 2019. Language variation policy in the Dutch language area. In T. Schoonheim, J. Van Hoorde (eds.), *Language Variation. A Factor of Increasing Complexity and A challenge for Language Policy Within Europe.* Budapest: Research Institute of Linguistics, Hungarian Academy of Sciences, 138–144.

Blommaert, Jan (ed.) 1999. *Language Ideological Debates.* Berlin, New York: Mouton De Gruyter.

Bokhorst-Heng, Wendy. 1999. Singapore's *Speak Mandarin-Campaign*: Language ideological debates and the imagining of the nation. In: J. Blommaert (ed.) *Language Ideological Debates.* Berlin, New York: Mouton De Gruyter, 235–265.

Bourdieu, Pierre. 1991. *Language and Symbolic Power.* Cambridge: Polity.

Bourgeois, Annie. 2023. Bill C-13: The Official Languages Act gets a revamp. LANGLOIS, 26 June. https://langlois.ca/bill-c-13-the-official-languages-act-gets-a-revamp/

Breton, Roland J.-L. 2000. Can English be dethroned? *The UNESCO Courier*, 17–36. https://unesdoc.unesco.org/ark:/48223/pf0000119482

Bromham, L., Dinnage, R., Skirgård, H. et al. 2022. Global predictors of language endangerment and the future of linguistic diversity. *Nature Ecology & Evolution* 6: 163–173. https://doi.org/10.1038/s41559-021-01604-y

Brook, Marisa. 2024. Sociolinguistics in Canada. In M.J. Ball, R. Mesthrie (eds.), *The Routledge Handbook of Sociolinguistics Around the World.* London: Routledge, Chapter 2.

Bruzos, Alberto, Iker Erdocia, Kamran Khan. 2018. The path to naturalization in Spain: Old ideologies, new language testing regimes and the problem of the test use. *Language Policy* 17: 419–441.

Caldas, Stephen J. 2012. Language policy in the family. In B. Spolsky (ed.), *The Cambridge Handbook of Language Policy*. Cambridge: Cambridge University Press, 351–373.

Cameron, Deborah. 1995. *Verbal Hygiene*. London: Routledge.

Cameron, Deborah. 1998. *The Feminist Critique of Language*, second edition. London and New York: Routledge.

Camut, Nicolas. 2023. UN experts slam Latvia for clamping down on Russian-language minorities. *Politico*, 8 February. https://www.politico.eu/article/united-nations-experts-latvia-russian-language-minorities/

Capstick, Tony. 2020. *Language and Migration*. London: Routledge.

Castles, Stephen and Alastair Davidson (eds.) 2000. *Citizenship and Migration Globalization and the Politics of Belonging*. New York: Routledge.

Chan, Kai. 2016. These are the most powerful languages in the world. *World Economic Forum*, 2 December. https://www.weforum.org/agenda/2016/12/these-are-the-most-powerful-languages-in-the-world/

Chen, Albert H.Y. 1998. The philosophy of language rights. *Language Sciences* 20: 45–54.

Climent-Ferrando, Vicent. 2023. Assessing the European Union's support to regional and minority languages 10 years after the Alfonsi Resolution (2013–2023). Parlement européen. https://www.izaskunbilbao.eus/download/Final_Report_RMLs_Climent.pdf

Çolak, Yilmaz. 2004. Language policy and official ideology in early republican Turkey. *Middle Eastern Studies* 40: 67–91.

Comrie, Bernard and Greville G. Corbett (eds.) 1993. *The Slavonic Languages*. London and New York: Routledge.

Confucius. 1992. *The Analects*. Translated by D.C. Lau. Hong Kong: The Chinese University Press.

Cooper, Robert L. 1989. *Language Planning and Social Change*. Cambridge: Cambridge University Press.

Coulmas, Florian. 1989. The surge of Japanese. *International Journal of the Sociology of Language* 80: 115–131. https://doi.org/10.1515/ijsl.1989.80.115

Coulmas, Florian. 1991. *A Language Policy for the EC*. Berlin: Mouton de Gruyter.

Coulmas, Florian. 1998. Language Rights—Interests of State, Language Groups and the Individual. *Language Sciences* 20: 63–72.

Coulmas, Florian. 2016. *Guardians of Language. Twenty Voices Through History*. Oxford: Oxford University Press.

Coulmas, Florian. 2019. *Identity. A Very Short Introduction*. Oxford: Oxford University Press.

Coulmas, Florian. 2023. Reading two books. Interalia Magazine, February. https://www.interaliamag.org/articles/florian-coulmas-reading-two-books/

Council of Europe. 2004. *The European Charter for Regional and Minority Languages and the French Dilemma: Diversity v. Unicity – Which Language for the Republic?* Strasbourg: Council of Europe.

Council of Europe. 2013. *Integration Tests: Helping or Hindering Integration*. Committee on Migration, Refugees and Displaced Persons. http://www.assembly.coe.int/CommitteeDocs/2013/amdoc11_2013TA.pdf

Council of Europe. 2014. Quality in the linguistic integration of adult migrants: from values to policy and practice. Report by Richard Rossner. Strasbourg: Language Policy Unit, Education Policy Division. https://rm.coe.int/0900001680305c65

Crawford, James. 2000. At war with diversity: U.S. language policy in an age of anxiety. *Multilingual Matters*. p. 17. ISBN 978-1-85359-505-9.

Crawley, Cheryl K. 2020. *Native American Bilingual Education (An Ethnography of Powerful Forces)*. Bingley: Emerald Publishing.

Darquennes, Jeroen. 2015. Language conflict research: a state of the art. *International Journal of the Sociology of Language* 235: 7–32. https://doi.org/10.1515/ijsl-2015-0012

de Groot, Gerard-René. 2019. European Charter for Regional and Minority Languages. In T. Schoonheim, J. Van Hoorde (eds.), *Language Variation. A Factor of Increasing Complexity and a Challenge for Language Policy Within Europe*. Budapest: Hungarian Academy of Sciences: 115–128.

De Keere, Kobe and Mark Elchardus. 2011. Narrating linguistic conflict: A storytelling analysis of the language conflict in Belgium. *Journal of Multilingual and Multicultural Development* 32: 221–234. DOI 10.1080/01434632.2011.563857

de Sola Pool, Ithiel. 1983. *Technologies of Freedom*. Cambridge, MA.: Harvard University Press.

de Souza, Andre Felix. 2022. Cosmopolis: public spaces, cosmopolitanism, and democracy. *GeoJournal*. http://orcid.org/0000-0003-0137-3493

De Swaan, Abram. 2001. *Words of the World*. Cambridge: Polity.

Dhir, Krishna S. 2019. Contribution of language to the creation of corporate social capital. *Revista Internacional de Organizaciones* 23: 243–263.

Díez, Beatriz. 2019. 'English Only': The movement to limit Spanish speaking in US. *BBC News* 3 December. https://www.bbc.com/news/world-us-canada-50550742

Djité, Paulin G. 2014. Language and development: theories and sobering realities. *International Journal of the Sociology of Language* 225: 147–161.

Dunant, Sarah (ed.) 1994. *The War of the Words. The Political Correctness Debate*. London: Virago Press.

Extra, Guus, Massimiliano Spotti, Piet Van Avermaet (eds.) 2009. *Language Testing, Migration and Citizenship: Cross-national Perspectives on Integration Regimes*. London: Continuum.

Feng, Cao. A New Examination of Confucius' Rectification of Names. *Journal of Chinese Humanities* 2/2: 147–171 (DOI: https://doi.org/10.1163/23521341-12340032)

Ferguson, Charles A. 1959. Diglossia. *Word* 15: 325–340.

Fichte, Johann Gottlieb. 1922 [1807/08]. *Reden an die Deutsche Nation*. English translation by R.F. Jones and G.R. Turnbull, *Addresses to the German Nation*. Chicago and London: The Open Court Publishing Co. Internet Archive: https://ia800201.us.archive.org/9/items/addressestogerma00fich/addressestogerma00fich.pdf

Fishman, Joshua. A. 1972. *The Sociology of Language*. Rowley: Newbury House.

Fukuyama, Francis. 2018. *Identity. The Demand for Dignity and the Politics of Resentment*. New York: Farrar, Straus and Giroux.

Gandhi, Mohandas K. 1965. *Our Language Problem*. Bombay: Bharatiya Vidya Bhavan (Pocket Gandhi Series No. 13).

Gazzola, Michele. 2016. *European Strategy for Multilingualism: Benefits and Costs*. European Parliament, Directorate-General for Internal Policies. https://www.europarl.europa.eu/RegData/etudes/STUD/2016/573460/IPOL_STU(2016)573460_EN.pdf

Gazzola, Michele and Bengt-Arne Wickström (eds.). 2016. *The Economics of Language Policy*. Cambridge, MA: MIT Press.

Geerts, Guido. 2011. Language legislation in Belgium and the balance of power in Walloon-Flemish relationships. In Roeland van Hout and Uus Knops (eds.), *Language Attitudes in the Dutch Language Area*. Berlin, New York: De Gruyter Mouton, 2011, pp. 25–38.

Goh, Yeng-Seng. 2017. Teaching Chinese as an International Language. A Singapore perspective. Cambridge: Cambridge University Press.

Griffiths, James. 2021. *Speak Not: Empire, Identity and the Politics of Language.* London: Bloomsbury.

Grin, François. 2005. Linguistic human rights as a source of policy guidelines: A critical assessment. *Journal of Sociolinguistics* 9: 448–460.

Grin, François, Claudio Sfreddo, François Vaillancourt. 2010. *The Economics of the Multilingual Workplace.* London: Routledge.

Habermas, Jürgen. 1991. *The Structural Transformation of the Public Sphere. An Inquiry into a Category of Bourgeois Society.* Translated by Thomas Burger. Cambridge, MA.: MIT Press.

Habermas, Jürgen. 2022. *Ein neuer Strukturwandel der Öffentlichkeit und die deliberative Politik.* Frankfurt: Suhrkamp.

Hamied, Fuad Abdul and Bachrudin Mustafa. 2019. Policies on language education in Indonesia. *Indonesian Journal of Applied Linguistics* 9: 308–315. http://ejournal.upi.edu/index.php/IJAL/article/view/20279

Haugen, Einar. 1959. Planning for a standard language in modern Norway. *Anthropological Linguistics* 1: 8–21. http://www.jstor.org/stable/30028247. Accessed 6 Aug. 2023

Heller, Monica. 2003. *Crosswords: Language, Education, and Ethnicity in French Ontario.* Berlin, New York: Mouton de Gruyter.

Heller, Monica. 2018. Socioeconomic junctures, theoretical shifts: A genealogy of language policy and planning research. In James W. Tollefson, and Miguel Pérez-Milans (eds.), *The Oxford Handbook of Language Policy and Planning*, online edn., https://doi.org/10.1093/oxfordhb/9780190458898.013.6

Heller, Monica. 2018b. *Language, skill and authenticity in the globalized new economy.* http://www.gencat.cat/llengua/noves/noves/hm05hivern/docs/heller.pdf

Hill, Loyd. 2010. Language and status: On the limits of language planning. *Stellenbosch Papers in Linguistics* 39: 41–58. Doi: 10.5774/39-0-3

Hogan-Brun, Gabrielle, Clinton Robinson, Ingo Thonhauser. 2013. Acquisition planning. In Carol A. Chapelle (ed.) *The Encyclopedia of Applied Linguistics.* DOI: 10.1002/9781405198431.wbeal0007

Hult, Francis M. and David Cassels Johnson (eds.) 2015. *Research Methods in Language Policy and Planning.* Oxford: Wiley Blackwell.

Jernudd, Björn and Jiří V. Neustupný. 1987. Language planning: For whom? In L. Laforge (ed.) *Proceedings of the International Colloquium on Language Planning.* Québec: Les Presses de L'Université Laval, 69–84.

Kamusella, Tomasz. 2010. Review: After Serbo-Croatian: The narcissism of small difference. *Polish Sociological Review* 171: 335–340.

Kamusella, Tomasz, Motoki Nomachi, and Catherine Gibson (eds.) 2015. *The Palgrave Handbook of Slavic Languages, Identities and Borders.* London: Palgrave.

Keen, Andrew. 2015. *The Internet Is Not the Answer.* New York: Gove Atlantic.

Kindleberger, Charles P. 1967. The politics of international money and world language. *Essays in International Finance*, 61: 1–11.

King, Kendall A., Lyn W, Fogle, and Aubrey Logan-Terry. 2008. Family language policy. *Language and Linguistics Compass* 2: 907–922.

Kirschner, Jonathan. 2003. Money is politics. *Review of International Political Economy* 10: 645–660.

Kloss, Heinz. 1966. German-American language maintenance efforts. In J.A. Fishman (ed.) *Language Loyalty in the United States.* The Hague: Mouton, 206–252.

Kloss, Heinz. 1967. Abstand languages and Ausbau languages. *Anthropological Linguistics* 9: 29–41.

Koffi, Ettien. 2012. *Paradigm Shift in Language Planning and Policy. Game-theoretic solutions.* Berlin, New York: De Gruyter Mouton.

Kraus, Peter A. and François Grin (eds.) 2018. *The Politics of Multilingualism. Europeanisation, Globalisation and Linguistic Governance.* Amsterdam: John Benjamins.

Kritikos, Georgios. 2013. The nationalism of Greek language: the two faces of Janus in the early twentieth century. *Balkan Studies* 47: 133–163. https://www.imxa.gr/files/bsfiles/47/Kritikos.pdf

Krogstad, Jens Manuel, Jeffrey S. Passel, and Luis Noe-Bustamante. 2022. Key facts about U.S. Latinos for National Hispanic Heritage Month. *Pew Research Center*, 23 September. https://www.pewresearch.org/short-reads/2022/09/23/key-facts-about-u-s-latinos-for-national-hispanic-heritage-month/

Kymlicka, Will. 2007. *Multicultural Odysseys: Navigating the New International Politics of Diversity.* Oxford: Oxford University Press.

Laitin, David D. 2000. What is a language community? *American Journal of Political Science* 44: 142–155.

Lasswell, Harold D. 1956. *The Decision Process: Seven Categories of Functional Analysis.* College Park: University of Maryland Press.

Leerkes, Arjen, Jaco Dagevos. 2016. Herziening van de termen 'autochtoon' en 'allochtoon' is nodig: afschaffen, hernoemen of herdefiniëren? *Sociale Vraagstukken.* https://www.socialevraagstukken.nl/herziening-van-de-termen-autochtoon-en-allochtoon-is-nodig-afschaffen-hernoemen-of-herdefinieren/

Leibowicz, Joseph. 1984. The Proposed English Language Amendment: Shield or Sword? *Yale Law & Policy Review* 3: 519–550. https://digitalcommons.law.yale.edu/ylpr/vol3/iss2/9.

Li Sizuan. 2021. China's Confucius Institute in Africa: a different story? *International Journal of Comparative Education and Development* 23: 353–366. https://doi.org/10.1108/IJCED-02-2021-0014

Li Yuming, Li Wei (eds.) 2014. *The Language Situation in China, vol.2.* Boston, Berlin: De Gruyter and Beijing: Commercial Press.

Lim, Lisa, Christopher Stroud, and Lionel Wee (eds.) 2018. *The Multilingual Citizen. Towards a Politics of Language for Agency and Change.* Bristol: Multilingual Matters.

Liu, Lu. 2018. 'It's Just Natural': A Critical Case Study of Family Language Policy in a 1.5 Generation Chinese Immigrant Family on the West Coast of the United States. In M. Siiner, F. Hult, T. Kupisch (eds.) *Language Policy and Language Acquisition Planning.* Springer, 13–31. https://doi.org/10.1007/978-3-319-75963-0_2

Lopes, Armando Jorge. 2004. The language situation in Mozambique. In Richard B. Baldauf Jr and Robert B. Kaplan (eds.) *Language Planning and Policy in Africa, Vol 1: Botswana, Malawi, Mozambique.* Bristol, Blue Ridge Summit: Multilingual Matters, 150–196. https://doi.org/10.21832/9781853597268-005

Lopez, Rachel. 2019. The Shocking Rise in Anti-Latino Hate Crimes. *Salud America!* 2 December. https://salud-america.org/the-shocking-rise-in-anti-latino-hate-crimes/

Loring, Ariel and Vaidehi Ramanthan (eds.) 2016. *Language, Immigration and Naturalization: Legal and Linguistic Issues.* Bristol: Multilingual Matters.

Lozinskiy, Nikolay. 2020. *Multilingualism in the United Nations System.* Geneva: United Nations. https://www.unjiu.org/sites/www.unjiu.org/files/jiu_rep_2020_6_english.pdf

Macías, R.F. 2014. Spanish as the Second National Language of the United States: Fact, Future, Fiction, or Hope? Review of Research in Education, 38(1), 33–57. https://doi.org/10.3102/0091732X13506544

Madumulla, Joshua, Elena Bertocini, and Jan Blommaert. 1999. Politics, ideology and poetic form: The literary debate in Tanzania. In J. Blommaert (ed.) *Language Ideological Debates*. Berlin, New York: Mouton De Gruyter, 307–341.

Makoni, Sinfree and Alastair Pennycook (eds.) 2007. *Disinventing and Reconstituting Languages*. Clevedon: Multilingual Matters.

Makoni, Sinfree, Busi Makoni, Ashraf Abdelhay. 2012. Colonial and post-colonial language policies in Africa: historical and emerging landscapes. In B. Spolsky (ed.). 2012. *The Cambridge Handbook of Language Policy*. Cambridge: Cambridge University Press, 523–543.

Makoni, Sinfree, Cristine Severo, and Ashraf Abdelhay. 2023. Postcolonial language policy and planning and the limits of the notion of the modern state. *Annual Review of Linguistics*. 2023. 9: 483–96. https://www.annualreviews.org/doi/pdf/10.1146/annurev-linguistics-030521-052930

Marçais, William. 1930. La diglossia arabe. *L'ensignement public* 97: 401–409.

Maxwell, Alexander. 2003. 'Literary dialects' in China and Slovakia: imagining unitary nationality with multiple orthographies. *International Journal of the Sociology of Language* 164: 129–149.

May, Stephen. 2023. Sociolinguistic and political theory perspectives on language rights. In T. Skutnabb-Kangas, R. Phillipson (eds.), *2023. The Handbook of Linguistic Human Rights*. Oxford: Wiley Blackwell, 39–54.

Mazzini, Giuseppe. 2005 [1860]. *The Duties of Man and other Essays*. New York: Cosimo.

Mazzon, Gabriella. 2022. 'Good Savage' vs. 'Bad Savage.' Discourse and counter-discourse on primitive language as a reflex of English colonialism. *Topoi* 41: 551–560. https://link.springer.com/article/10.1007/s11245-021-09743-4

Michel, Marije, Christine Vidon, Rick de Graaff, and Wander Lowie. 2020. Language Learning beyond English in the Netherlands: A fragile future? *European Journal of Applied Linguistics* https://doi.org/10.1515/eujal

Mignolo, Walter. 2001. Géopolitique de la connaissance, colonialité de pouvoir e difference colonial. *Multitudes*, Septembre, 56–71.

Mills, Sara. 2008. *Language and Sexism*. Cambridge: Cambridge University Press.

Moens, Barbara and Aitor Hernández-Morales. 2023. Doubts over Catalan as EU language create a headache for Spain's Sánchez. *Politico*, 8 September. https://www.politico.eu/article/catalonia-eu-language-pedro-sanchez-spain-socialist-party/

Montolalu, Lucy R. and Leo Suryadinata. 2015. National language and nation-building: The case of Bahasa Indonesia. In *Language, Nation and Development in Southeast Asia* (Lectures, Workshops, and Proceedings of International Conferences, pp. 39–50). ISEAS–Yusof Ishak Institute.

Mori, Soya and Sugimoto, Atsubumi. 2019. Progress and problems in the 'campaign for sign language recognition in Japan.' In M. De Meulder, J.J. Murray, and R.L. McKee (eds.), *The Legal Recognition of Sign Languages: Advocacy and Outcomes Around the World*. Bristol, Blue Ridge Summit: Multilingual Matters, 104–118. https://doi.org/10.21832/9781788924016-008

Motschenbacher, Heiko. 2014. Grammatical gender as a challenge for language policy: The (im)possibility of non-heteronormative language use in German versus English. *Language Policy* 13: 243–261.

Mühlhäusler, Peter and Rom Harré. 1990. *Pronouns and People. The Linguistic Construction of Personal Identity*. Oxford: Basil Blackwell.

Nadeau, Serge. 2009. Another Look at the Francophone Wage Gap in Canada: Public vs Private Sector, Quebec vs Outside Quebec. *WORKING PAPER #0912E*, Department of Economics, University of Ottawa. https://sciencessociales.uottawa.ca/economics/sites/socialsciences.uottawa.ca.economics/files/0912E.pdf (accessed 10 August 2023)

NALEO Educational Fund. 2020. 2020 Census Profiles Florida https://naleo.org/wp-content/uploads/2021/12/2020-Census-Profiles-FL.pdf

Newland, Bryan. 2022. *Federal Indian Boarding School Initiative Investigative Report.* https://www.bia.gov/sites/default/files/dup/inline-files/bsi_investigative_report_may_2022_508.pdf

Oakes, Leigh. 2017. Normative language policy and minority language rights: rethinking the case of regional languages in France. *Language Policy* 16: 365–384.

Pattanayak, Debi P. 1998. Mother tongue: An Indian context. In Rajendra Singh (ed.) *The Native Speaker. Multilingual Perspectives.* New Delhi, Thousand Oaks, London: Sage, 125–147.

Patten, Allan and Will Kymlicka. 2003. Introduction: Language rights and political theory. In A. Patten, W. Kymlicka (eds.), *Language Rights and Political Theory.* Oxford: Oxford University Press, 1–31.

Pauwels, Anne. 2013. Politics of Multilingualism. *SOAS online lecture.* https://www.soas.ac.uk/about/event/prof-anne-pauwels-inaugural-lecture-politics-multilingualism-and-language-learning-who

Petričević, Vanja. 2015. *Compliance Patterns with European Union Anti-Discrimination Legislation.* London: Palgrave Macmillan.

Phillipson, Robert. 1992. *Linguistic Imperialism.* New York: Oxford University Press.

Plato. 2005. *Phaedrus.* Translated by Benjamin Jowett. A Digireads.com book, 2005. Internet Archive.

Pool, Jonathan. 1972. National development and language diversity. In Joshua Fishman (ed.) *Advances in the Sociology of Language,* vol. 2, 213–230. The Hague: Mouton.

Potowski, Kim and Maria Carreira. 2012. Spanish in the USA. In Kim Potowski (ed.) *Language Diversity in the USA.* Cambridge: Cambridge University Press, 66–80. doi.org/10.1017/CBO9780511779855.005

Pullum, Geoffrey K. 1991. Here come the linguistic fascists. In *The Great Eskimo Vocabulary Hoax and Other Irreverent Essays on the Study of Language.* Chicago: University of Chicago Press, 111–19.

Radtke, Edgar, Sybille Große, Ekkehard Felder, Ronja Grebe. 2019. Language institutions and language criticism in European perspective. *Handbuch Europäische Sprachkritik Online,* vol. 4, Sprachinstitutionen und Sprachkritik. https://doi.org/10.17885/heiup.heso.2019.1.24071

Rahman, Jacquelyn. 2012. The N word: Its history and use in the African-American community. *Journal of English Linguistics* 40: 137–171. https://doi.org/10.1177%2F0075424211414807

Rehg, Kenneth L. and Lyle Campbell (eds.) *2018. The Oxford Handbook of Endangered Languages.* Oxford: Oxford University Press.

Ricento, Thomas. 2000. Historical and theoretical perspectives in language policy and planning. *Journal of Sociolinguistics* 4: 196–213.

Ricento, Thomas. 2012. Political economy and English as a 'global' language. *Critical Multilingualism Studies* 1: 31–56.

Ricento, Thomas, Yael Peled, and Peter Ives (eds.) 2014. Language Policy and Political Theory. *Language Policy* 13:4 (special issue).

Robins, Robert H. and Eugenius M. Uhlenbeck (eds.) 1991. *Endangered Languages.* Oxford: Berg.

Robitaille, Louis-Bernard. 2002. *Le Salon des immortels: une académie très française.* Paris: Denoël.

Rohsenow, John S. 2004. Fifty years of script and written language reform in the P.R.C. In Minglang Zhou and Hongkai Sun (eds.), 2004. *Language Policy in the People's Republic of China. Theory and Practice since 1949*. Boston: Kluwer Academic Publishers, 21–43.

Romaine, Suzanne. 2009. Linguistic diversity and poverty: Many languages and poor people in a globalizing world. In Li Wei (ed.) *Contemporary Applied Linguistics, Volume 2 Linguistics for the Real World*. New York: Continuum, 46–64.

Ryan, Alan. 2012. *On Politics: A History of Political Thought from Herodotus to the Present*. London: Allen Lane.

Sassen, Saskia. 2010. Reading the city in a global digital age: The limits of topographic representation. *Procedia Social and Behavioral Sciences* 2: 7030–7041 https://doi.org/10.1016/j.sbspro.2010.05.057

Schiffman, Harold (ed.). 2011. Language Policy and Language Conflict in Afghanistan and Its Neighbors. Leiden: Brill. Review Language Policy 12/4 2013 https://brill.com/view/title/17296

Seals, Corinne A. 2019. *Choosing a Mother Tongue: The Politics of Language and Identity in Ukraine*. Bristol: Channel View Publications.

Shandilya, Marisha and Nidhi Kumari. 2022. Cyber Space and the various Challenges attached to the regulation of Information and Communication Technology. *Law Panch*, 2 March. https://lawpanch.com/cyber-space-and-the-various-challenges-attached-to-the-regulation-of-information-and-communication-technology-%EF%BF%BC/

Sheffer, Gabriel. 2003. *Diaspora Politics. At Home Abroad*. Cambridge: Cambridge University Press.

Shohamy, Elana and T. McNamara. 2009. Language tests for citizenship, immigration, and asylum. *Language Assessment Quarterly* 6: 1–5.

Shohamy, Elana. 2006. *Language Policy: Hidden Agendas and New Approaches*. London: Routledge.

Shohamy, Elana. 2023. Language testing/assessment and linguistic human rights. In T. Skutnabb-Kangas, R. Phillipson (eds.), 2023. *The Handbook of Linguistic Human Rights*. Oxford: Wiley Blackwell, 605–612.

Sibomana, Emmanuel. 2015. Postcolonial language-in-education policies in Africa: The case of Kenya. *Rwandan Journal of Education* 3: 37–51.

Skutnabb-Kangas, Tove and Robert Phillipson (eds.) 1995. *Linguistic Human Rights. Overcoming Linguistic Discrimination*. Berlin, New York: Mouton de Gruyter.

Skutnabb-Kangas, Tove and Robert Phillipson (eds.) 2023. *The Handbook of Linguistic Human Rights*. Oxford: Wiley Blackwell.

Spolsky, Bernard (ed.). 2012. *The Cambridge Handbook of Language Policy*. Cambridge: Cambridge University Press.

Stickel, Gerhard (ed.) 2018. *National language institutions and national languages. Contributions to the EFNIL Conference 2017 in Mannheim*. Budapest: Research Institute for Linguistics, Hungarian Academy of Sciences. Accessible through the EFNIL website at: http://www.efnil.org

Stroud, Christopher. 2018. Introduction. In Lisa Lim, Christopher Stroud, Lionel Wee (eds.), 2018. *The Multilingual Citizen. Towards a politics of language for agency and change*. Bristol: Multilingual Matters, 1–14.

Sutherland, William J. 2003. Parallel extinction risk and global distribution of languages and species. *Nature* 423: 276–279.

Terasawa, Takunori. 2018. Evidence-based language policy: theoretical and methodological examination based on existing studies. *Current Issues in Language Planning* 20: 1–21. 10.1080/14664208.2018.1495372}

Terra, Sandra Elena L. 2021. Bilingual education in Mozambique: a case-study on educational policy, teacher beliefs, and implemented practices. *International Journal of Bilingual Education and Bilingualism* 24: 16–30. https://doi.org/10.1080/13670050.2018.1441803

Thomas, George. 1991. *Linguistic Purism*. London: Longman.

Tollefson, James W., Miguel Pérez-Milans (eds.) 2018. *The Oxford Handbook of Language Policy and Planning*. Oxford: Oxford University Press.

UNESCO Atlas of the World's Languages in danger. http://www.unesco.org/languages-atlas

UNESCO. 2005. Guidelines for Terminology Policies: Formulating and Implementing Terminology Policy in Language Communities. International Information Centre for Terminology (Austria). https://unesdoc.unesco.org/ark:/48223/pf0000140765

Ura, Alexa. 2023. Hispanics officially make up the biggest share of Texas' population, new census numbers show. *The Texas Tribune*, June 21. https://www.texastribune.org/2023/06/21/census-texas-hispanic-population-demographics/

Van der Horst, Joop. 2008. *Het Einde van de Standaardtaal. Een wisseling van Europese taalcultuur*. Amsterdam: Meulenhoff.

Van Parijs, Philippe. 2011. *Linguistic Justice for Europe and the World*. Oxford: Oxford University Press.

Wąsikiewicz-Firlej, Emilia, and Michelle Daly. 2013. Family language policy in the context of return migration: A case study. *Glottodidactica* 50: 213–241. Doi.org/10.14746/gl.2023.50.1.11

Watson, J.K.P. 1983. Cultural pluralism, nation-building and education policies in peninsular Malaysia. In C. Kennedy (eds.), *Language Planning and Language Education*. London: George Allen & Unwin, 133–150.

Weber, Max. 1968 [1921]. *Economy and Society. An Outline of Interpretive Sociology*. Berkeley: University of California Press.

Weinstein, Brian. 1983. *The Civic Tongue. Political Consequences of Language Choices*. New York, London: Longman.

Woolard, Kathryn A. 2020. Language ideology. In James Stanlaw (ed.) *The International Encyclopedia of Linguistic Anthropology*. https://doi.org/10.1002/9781118786093.iela0217

Wright, Sue. 2015. What is a language? A response to Philippe van Parijs. *Critical Review of International Social and Political Philosophy* 18: 113–130. https://doi.org/10.1080/13698230.2015.1023628

Yao, Don and Matthew P. Wallace. 2021. Language Assessment for Immigration: A Review of Validation Research Over the Last Two Decades. *Frontiers in Psychology* 11. https://www.frontiersin.org/articles/10.3389/fpsyg.2021.773132/full

Yuan, Z., J. Guo, and H. Zhu. 2016. Confucius Institutes and the limitations of China's global cultural network. *China Information* 30: 334–356. https://doi.org/10.1177/0920203X16672167

Zhou, Minglang. 2004. Minority language policy in China. In Minglang Zhou and Hongkai Sun (eds.) *Language Policy in the People's Republic of China. Theory and Practice Since* 1949. Boston: Kluwer, 71–95.

Zhou, Minglang and Hongkai Sun (eds.) 2004. *Language Policy in the People's Republic of China. Theory and Practice Since 1949*. Boston: Kluwer Academic Publishers.

Zuckerman, Ethan. 2013. *Digital Cosmopolitans. Why We Think the Internet Connects Us, Why It Doesn't, and How to Rewire It*. New York: W.W. Norton.

Index

For the benefit of digital users, indexed terms that span two pages (e.g., 52–53) may, on occasion, appear on only one of those pages.